VEGAN · ORGANIC · SUSTAINABLE

G·ZEN

PEACE BEGINS ON YOUR PLATE

Shadlefarm art work by Vasilisa Romanenko

Published by Peaceful Daily
www.peacefuldaily.com

Library of Congress Control Number:
2018964662

ISBN 978-0-9982579-9-0

Book design by Pettus Creative, www.pettuscreative.com
Photos by Jeff Skeirik aka Rawtographer

Printed in the United States of America.

FIRST EDITION

10 9 8 7 6 5 4 3 2 1

Peace begins on your plate

VEGAN • ORGANIC • PLANT-BASED

By Chef Ami Beach & Chef Mark Shadle and special guests

LOVE, SERVE, REMEMBER
– Ram Das

Peace Begins on Your Plate

By Chef Ami Beach & Chef Mark Shadle and special guests

This book is dedicated to all Animals of the Planet.

Giving a voice to those creatures without a voice and embodying
"Ahimsa" as a spiritual path.

> **Ahimsa**: Non-violence or non-injury; Ahimsa is an attitude of harmlessness and a feeling of universal benevolence and compassion for all Living creatures, Planet Earth and Mother Nature as a whole.

Endorsement from Anthony William

"Chefs Mark Shadle and Ami Beach are true innovators of first-class, plant-based cuisine. In G-Zen's "Peace Begins on Your Plate," they lovingly show you how to create a collection of their life-enhancing recipes that are as vibrant and delicious as they are healthy."

Anthony William, Medical Medium, *New York Times* best-selling author

As we go through life, there is great demand upon us to focus on surviving the weight of our responsibilities and day-to-day pressures. As children, much of our time and attention is directed towards getting through school. After that, most of our time is spent learning new terrain, adjusting and acclimating constantly. Then, as we grow older, we focus on developing trustful and reliable friendships while we search for a soul mate in life, perhaps forging ahead and building a family with that person. We work so we can do our best to keep ourselves and our loved ones fed, sheltered and cared for, sometimes in jobs we would prefer to never do, and other times in jobs we enjoy, but have other kinds of pressures. Through all the experiences we endure and all the battles we face, we are forced to grow, learn, survive, and rise above our hardships.

There are so many meaningful pieces of our lives that we must vigilantly protect as we move through life, and as we're doing that, one critical element seems to be getting pushed aside, ignored and forgotten. It's real food, which is different than the food we normally choose for day-to-day survival. What we eat plays an unimaginably essential role in who we are, who we are becoming and where we are going, individually and together as humankind.

Real food is vital and life protecting. It contains its own intrinsic wisdom, the power and essence of which is still largely undiscovered. We can waste decades of our lives eating harmful foods — and they are not just the processed foods most people consider unhealthy. There are other foods widely lauded as nutritious that are actually damaging to our health and well-being. These foods can be tricky to identify because they seem so normal in today's eating culture. They are often found even on the shelves of health food stores. Knowing which foods serve us in our lifetime and which do not is critical.

As we fight our battles and persevere through our journeys in life, years may go by where we fuel ourselves with foods that don't offer us the best support for our time here on Earth. We don't give our bodies the foods that can provide us with a coat of armor against illness and disease and allow us to embrace full, vibrant lives. Instead, we knowingly or unknowingly choose foods that weigh against us, adding more burden and hardship, and detracting from the healthful, flourishing lives we desire and deserve, taking away a chance to grow younger in our years versus older in despair.

Unfortunately, caring for ourselves and preventing illness and disease through the foods we choose to eat is not taught to many of us or made a priority, even in today's world where countless cookbooks, cooking shows, health-driven communities and literature are surfacing on how to eat healthy. Many people don't ever consider how the foods they consume every day impact their bodies. Some people may experience "food numbness" or "food boredom" and no longer cherish or find joy in what they eat. Even if we know in our hearts the importance of the foods we consume, we lead busy lives and it's easy to lose our innate connection with what's really good for us. Oftentimes, things we value and appreciate can fall to the wayside among the challenges of life, and life-giving foods can be one of them. It's critical that we shift the relationship we have with the foods that nourish our body and arm us against illness, disease, contaminates, poisons and environmental toxins. We must begin to cherish the foods that keep us alive and fortified on our journey — real foods, like fruits, vegetables and leafy greens.

I've been to a lot of healthy restaurants over the years and tasted a lot of creative dishes made out of all varieties of produce, but I will never forget the day I walked into G-Zen — it felt different instantly. There was no emptiness or attitude to the atmosphere, the experience or the food. The restaurant was warm and real, created by people who really care — Chefs Mark Shadle and Ami Beach. Catching a glimpse of a few of G-Zen's incredible dishes, I knew this restaurant and its food was special. The inviting dishes held something that was alien to me — something different than the meals I'd had at all other first-rate restaurants.

These dishes had soul. Each dish was cared for and prepared with more than just passion. I've heard the word "passion" thrown around a lot in the health scene. Someone may have passion in something or a passion for what he or she does. And I believe that passion is important and truly matters. But, there was more than just passion involved with the foods that surrounded me at G-Zen. These dishes I was enjoying had compassion. I was deeply nourished by these compassion-filled foods, and there was an energy placed into these dishes that offered heart, soul, love and compassion to anyone who consumed them. Combined with incredible flavor, the experience and meal were unforgettable. I am honored to say that I believe this book you are about to read and enjoy holds within its pages and recipes that same very deeply compassionate nature that I personally experienced.

I am so thrilled that Chef Mark and Chef Ami are now bringing their combined creative inspiration to your table with this book of compassionate and light-filled recipes. In the pages that follow, you will find recipes for real food that give life, rather than taking it from you. Your senses will be engaged, your palate will be delighted, and the inherent healing and life-giving properties of the foods used will deeply support you on your journey. This is truly what I call a safe haven of light to help assist you to rise above, stronger.

Anthony William, *Medical Medium*

Notes of Gratitude and Thankfulness

We would like to give a very special thanks to the wonderful and supportive community of friends and family that surrounds G-Zen and our plant-based mission.

First and foremost, we would like to thank our devoted G-Zen staff for helping carry the torch while we are busy with this larger-than-life mission. We acknowledge all your efforts both individually and as a collective team; we love and appreciate every one of you. Without your support and hard work, we would not be able to touch as many lives with our important mission. Thank you for believing in our vision of a sustainable and vegan future.

Anthony William "Medical Medium," you will always be our soul brother. We have such respect for all the tireless and selfless work you do for healing others and the planet. You inspire us daily and we love you from the bottom of our hearts. Thank you for all your great wisdom and guidance from spirit. We are grateful to have you in our lives. The world is a better place knowing you are here to help guide us with your intuition and special gifts. The foreword to this book was so beautifully stated, deep and profound, and we couldn't have asked for a more perfect intro to this book. We are so honored to have you be a part of it and call you a dear friend.

Mimi Kirk & Mike Mendell, we cannot express how much it means to us to know we have your loyalty, friendship and support. We may not be close in miles, but our hearts are near and dear, always and forever. Meeting you both has forever touched our lives on a deep level. Keep on shining like the sun.

Dr. Ann Louise Gittleman, we respect you deeply and are so honored to call you not only a friend, but also a mentor on so many levels. Your unwavering support for our work means so much to both of us.

Priscilla Feral, President of Friends of Animals, your tireless commitment to animal liberation and equality is astounding. It is people like you that truly give a voice for the animals. We commend you on your work in the world and everything you represent.

Chef Bun Lai, we appreciate the authenticity and passion that goes into your life's work, your mission at Miya's and on a personal level. We will always be here to help one another to continue to raise the bar and help create a more sustainable world together.

To our Raw Sisters:

Muneeza Akhtar Ahmed, Rachel Feldman, Dara Dubinet, Valerie Lambert and Rhia Cataldo: Each of you is a fearless force of nature who radiates such divine love, joy and beauty in the world. We are honored to know such fiercely strong women, who are so beautiful inside and out. Thank you for helping shift the consciousness of the planet by sharing your unique gifts with all of us. Your high vibrations lift the energies of those around you, merely by your presence.

Rock on, sisters!

Special thanks to Sandy Corso at Peaceful Daily, Gina Ledwith at Holistically Well, Chris Dyer, Jeff Skeirik aka Rawtographer, Gabrielle Brick, Katrina Mayer and Vasi Romanenko for adding your creative talents and helping make this little book so special.

An extra special thanks to:

James Pettus at Pettus Creative for your brilliant design and branding of our "G" empire. We would not be here without you!

To our friends and family members on the East and West coasts of the USA, Canada and Culebra, PR and around the world, we thank you for your love and support. To our friends involved with animal welfare, activism and charity work for the animals, we love you all and appreciate your efforts so much.

Douglas & Margaret Beach, who have been a tremendous support for our vision thank you so very much.

Bruce Beach, thank you for finding our beautiful location in Branford, CT. We adore and love you.

Sal Annunziato, thank you for encouraging us to take a chance on Branford and shining your light our way.

Ryan & Caity Chabot for helping keep our G-Universe running and all the love you share with us.

Tyler Beach for your undying support and love for our vegan mission.

In loving memory of Steve MacDonald and Carol and Gordon Shadle, you will live on forever in our hearts.

To our spiritual teacher Shri Anandima, you are forever guiding towards the path of love and peace on Earth. Om shanti shanti.

A huge shout out to Chef Michael Richotte, Chef Stacy Attenberg, Courtney Rekos and the entire kitchen crew, as well as Sabrina Granniss, Sage Annunziato and the other warriors of light and love in the front of the house.

And last but not least, to our fans, customers and community, we love you dearly.

To anyone we haven't mentioned, you have not been forgotten in spirit.

In Love and Gratitude,

Ami & Mark

Table of Contents

"Let food be thy medicine and medicine be thy food."
Hippocrates

ABOUT MARK SHADLE

There is no path to peace,
peace is the path.

– GHANDI

Conscious Living by G-Zen

Mankind, in this modern day, has become further and further removed from living life the way nature intended. We have become less intuitive, less spontaneous and less connected to what our bodies want and need. The world is moving lightning fast and information is coming at us from every direction. Our central nervous systems are in overdrive and we are taking in toxins in our food, water and atmosphere that are being absorbed into our precious bodies faster than we can eliminate them. We have completely lost touch with what's important and somehow have made keeping up with technology more important than nurturing our bodies and caring for our families in the way nature intended. It's time to dial it back to the basics for the good of humankind and shift into a plant-based, holistic mentality.

Conscious living starts with the desire to make compassionate choices that create a healthy future for yourself, for the generations that follow you, for the greater good of the planet and for the animals. Making these changes can be difficult, especially when the world around you seems to be doing the opposite. You need to be the beacon of light that helps shift the old paradigm.

The impact of our society's eating habits is playing a tremendous role in the deterioration of our health and the environment. Packaged, processed, genetically modified, pesticide-laden foods are a far cry from what nature intended for us. We need to get back to supporting our local organic farmers and eating real, fresh, non-genetically modified foods that don't support animal farming/factory farming in any way. We need to start demanding that these organic foods are available at our local grocery stores and not just settle for the foods being offered. When possible, we strongly urge you to join your local CSA or community organic farm share. Or join forces with your neighbors and start your own garden and start empowering yourselves by growing your own medicinal foods.

Moving toward a pure plant-based diet that is organic whenever possible is the most direct path to healing the environment, our families and ourselves. We are here to help spread the message that the vegan path provides the greatest healing for our lives, our families and for the planet as a whole.

Peace Begins On Your Plate

The 4 Basic Principles of the G-Zen Lifestyle

G – Gratitude & Grace are absolutely vital for achieving your ideal life. Be grateful for the blessings in your life on a daily basis — for the food, air and water you drink. Be grateful for the friends, loved ones and animals that make our world such a special place. Maintaining a state of Gratitude & Grace throughout your day will literally help you heal on a physical, mental and emotional level.

G – Green Lifestyle and 100% organic and plant-based foods are crucial for maintaining vitality, ageless beauty and optimal radiant health. By choosing sustainability in all areas of your life and by making more conscious lifestyle choices, you will move closer to manifesting the life you've always dreamed of.

L – Vitamin "L" is the secret ingredient that is essential for our body to thrive. Every time you prepare your food or drink, intentionally add your Love and Intentions. It is a proven fact that your body assimilates and digests effectively when you put good ole' fashioned love into the food.

O – Oneness & Community will ultimately heal the planet and all of its inhabitants. Following these basic principles will allow you to share your unique gifts with others and with the world—all while living a life full of Passion, Health, Vitality and Purpose!

It's that simple!

The G-Zen Mission

It is our hearts' pure passion to share the joy of plant-based cuisine with as many people as we can reach. We wanted to thank you for taking the time to read "G-Zen Peace Begins on Your Plate" raw and cooked recipe book. It is our life's work to inspire people to attain the life and high level of health that they always dreamed of through the power of plant based-foods.

By embracing the power of a conscious and vegan diet, you will begin to see your life evolve in ways you didn't think were possible. It is not a lifestyle of restrictions; it is a lifestyle that is full of outrageous abundance, exotic tastes, endless possibilities and some of the most powerful tools for conquering your health, attaining your ideal body and manifesting the life that you know you deserve.

The key to unlocking the secrets of health and longevity lies in living as closely connected to nature as possible. A plant-based lifestyle is not simply about the food we eat, but also uncovering and exploring our authentic selves. The closer we can come to eating a purely plant-based diet, the more our bodies can fully thrive and heal, thus unleashing our passion and beauty from within. From this place, we are free to manifest and create a life full of vitality and purpose that is always connected to nature's inherent wisdom.

The recipes in this book are meant to show anyone and everyone that plant-based cuisine can be fun, simple and incredibly satisfying. Whether you are 100% vegan, aspire to be vegan or are just interested in adding healthier vegan options in your day-to-day life, these recipes can demonstrate how doable,

approachable and empowering it can be, no matter what your skill level is in the kitchen. You don't have to be a trained chef in order to feel like a rock star in the kitchen.

The recipes we have included are some of our random raw and cooked "all-time favorites" that we use both at home and at the restaurant! You will find many of these items on our regular menu, as regular specials or they may just be personal favorites of ours that we wanted to share with you. Sometimes just one or two simple, useful recipes can make a dramatic difference in your day-to-day life.

We have included a few life-changing recipes from our celebrity chef friends and colleagues who are leaders in the longevity, sustainability and holistic wellness arena. We hope to motivate you to take the first steps toward vibrant health and empower you to take charge of your destiny by creating a solid foundation of useful plant-based recipes that anybody can follow and master.

We highly suggest using as many 100% organic or biodynamic ingredients as possible when creating these recipes. At G-Zen, we aim to use 100% organic ingredients whenever possible. However, we fully understand that may not be possible in all circumstances, so please just do your best.

 Remember Vitamin "L" is the key ingredient. **LOVE.** We offer these recipes with Love and Gratitude.

Ami Beach & Mark Shadle

Kitchen Essentials

The few recommended essential kitchen tools we suggest having on hand for the raw recipes included in this book are:

- High-speed blender/Vitamix®
- Food dehydrator
- Food processor
- Mandoline food slicer & peeler
- Juicer

Feel free to make modifications if you don't have any of the above kitchen tools. For example, if you don't have a food dehydrator, you can use your oven turned to a low setting instead. The results may not be as ideal, but will still be tasty!

Please note: We do not specify serving sizes with our recipes since serving sizes can vary from person to person and with plant-based foods you can enjoy larger portions without any of the guilt.

Please feel free to omit, substitute or add any ingredients due to dietary restrictions or individual tastes.

* Please note that we have clearly marked the recipes that are **gluten-free, nut-free** and **raw**. The majority of the recipes in this book are naturally soy-free. However, any recipes that are not, can easily be made gluten-free or soy-free. By making a few adjustments or omitting one simple ingredient, you can make most of these recipes work for your dietary needs.

** For people who are soy sensitive, in any of our recipes that call for soy-based tamari or Bragg® Liquid Aminos, please substitute coconut aminos, which can be found at most health food stores, grocery stores or online.

Peace, Love and Vegan
Now Let's Rock!

Just get into the kitchen and have fun exploring these simple yet life changing plant-based recipes from our Hearts to Yours!

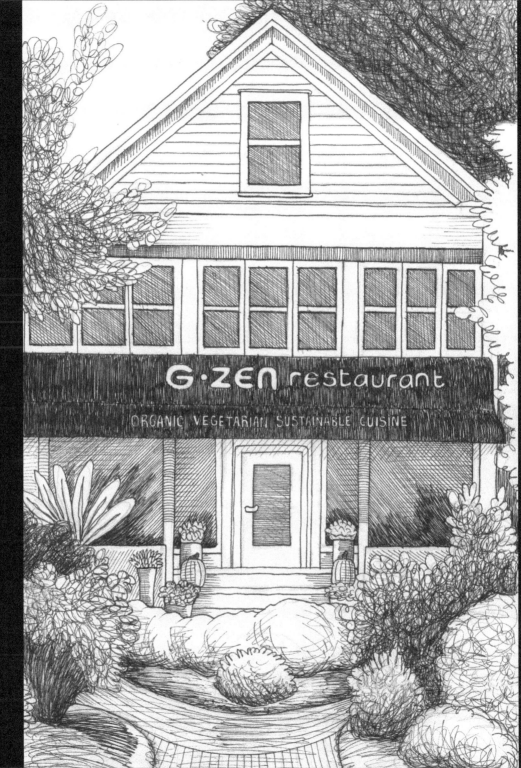

About G-Zen

G-Zen, in Branford, CT, opened in 2011 and is the **CT shoreline's premiere 100% vegan restaurant**, representing the vision of Master Chef Mark Shadle and Chef Ami Beach, both of whom have always been proponents of a sustainable & vegan lifestyle. For more than three decades, they have supported this movement and believe that the most important element is organic, seasonal, local food prepared in a flavorful, balanced way, hence the G-Zen name.

G-Zen was named among the **Top Ten Vegan** restaurants in America by the prestigious *Travel + Leisure* magazine and the **Food Network**. The restaurant was was given the **"Green Plate" award** by **The Nature Conservancy** as CT's most sustainable restaurant.

In addition to numerous other awards, G-Zen was featured in **Happy Cow's "Top Vegan Restaurants Around the World"** cookbook, representing the USA as one of the best of the best worldwide.

Friends of Animals praised G-Zen among the "Top 8 Vegan Restaurants in the USA."

The prestigious *New York Times* called G-Zen a "Vegan retreat for carnivores."

Executive Chef Mark Shadle is a pioneer of organic, environmentally conscious cuisine, both locally and internationally. The restaurant sources many of its organic ingredients from their own farm called Shadle Farm in Durham, CT, making it the only vegan restaurant in CT offering **"seed to table"** cuisine

from their own organic farm. G-Zen offers full-service dining with an extensive menu of gourmet, plant-based cuisine and raw foods, as well as organic beers, wine and botanical sake cocktails.

G-Zen is considered a zero-waste restaurant and composts 100% of its food waste at Shadle Farm, which is exclusively powered by solar energy. In addition, the restaurant uses fully compostable to-go containers, straws and napkins made from natural plant fibers. All of the furniture in the dining room is made from reclaimed barn wood and is hand-made by local artisans.

Many award-winning authors, celebrities, musicians and longevity leaders have made G-Zen a "must stop" destination when they are on the East coast.

VIP guests include Dr. Ann Louise Gittleman, Ph.D.; Anthony William, aka, Medical Medium; David "Avocado" Wolfe; Mimi Kirk; Dr. Caldwell Esselstyn featured in "Forks Over Knives,"; and Senator Ted Kennedy, Jr.

G-Zen is a sophisticated, yet relaxed sanctuary located in the charming shoreline town of Branford, CT. Located near the breathtaking Thimble Islands, the quaint village of Stony Creek and only minutes from downtown New Haven, the restaurant has become a refuge for many seeking sustainable, organic and vegan-friendly food along the CT coastline and "foodies" traveling between Boston and NYC.
www.g-zen.com

1730s Shadle Farm Green House, by Chris Dyer

7 Reasons to Consume Green Juice Every Day

1. Ensures absorption of nutrients – Fresh-pressed juice is easily absorbed into our bodies as it breaks down the cell walls of fruits and vegetables so that they are pre-digested for us. This means that the power-packed nutrients are going directly into your digestive system and flooding your cells and organs with plant enzymes immediately.

2. Ensures you will eat more greens – Juicing is a wonderful way to ensure that we are consuming our recommended servings of greens. It's a lot easier to drink a cup of celery juice rather than crunching through a whole bunch of celery. Juicing also allows you to consume a wide variety of healing greens all at once with the addition of others you probably wouldn't prepare to eat such as kale, cucumber, celery and parsley. And it's a great way to get children to eat more vegetables, which is so beneficial for their health.

3. Loads up the chlorophyll – Chlorophyll is what makes plants vibrant green in color, and is a very powerful element in nature. Chlorophyll not only cleanses the blood of impurities, but also builds up the blood with important nutrients that help to increase our circulation so we feel more energetic.

4. Boosts your trace minerals – Green juice is a great way to get all of the minerals that are vital to vibrant health and strengthening your immune system. Ensuring you get your daily essential minerals will mean that your body is better equipped to fight diseases and feel fabulous every day.

5. Releases toxins and maintains enzymes – The chlorophyll helps to release toxins from our bodies, which helps to cleanse, detoxify and renew at a cellular level. Cooking and processing of any type of vegetable destroys enzymes, so raw food, especially greens, is absolutely essential to maintain healthy enzyme levels.

6. Freshens breath – Not only do green juices enrich your blood with special nutrients that build iron, they also cleanse and improve the health of the intestines, liver and lungs. Green juice has been known to be beneficial as a natural breath freshener and body deodorizer.

7. Makes greens taste great – Juicing can make greens more palatable. By mixing organic greens with apples, carrots or other fruits, you can enjoy all of the benefits and alkalizing effects of greens while enjoying a delicious and satisfying drink.

Alkalizing Green Vitality Juice

(RAW, GLUTEN-FREE AND NUT-FREE)

Ingredients:

6 stalks celery

2 carrots

1 cucumber

¼ head green cabbage

1 cup kale or spinach

Small handful cilantro

½ lime

½ lemon

1 knob ginger

1 green apple, optional

Method:

1. Juice all ingredients using a vegetable juicer.

2. Gently mix juice together and consume immediately.

This is a wonderful green juice that helps balance the pH of the cells of the body and bloodstream. An over-acidic body is when we are prone to imbalances and diseases. The more alkaline foods we consume, especially from green juices, the better we can help keep the body strong and revitalized.

Apple Cider Vinaigrette

*G-ZEN FAVORITE
(GLUTEN-FREE AND NUT-FREE)

Ingredients:

2 apples, unpeeled and roughly chopped

¾ cup raw apple cider vinegar

1 cup apple juice

1 teaspoon garlic powder

½ medium red onion, chopped or diced

⅓ cup raw agave or maple syrup

2 tablespoons mustard powder

½ teaspoon sea salt

½ teaspoon pepper

1 cup extra-virgin olive oil

Method:

1. In a high-speed blender, blend all ingredients, except for the oil, until smooth.

2. While still blending, slowly drizzle in olive oil and blend well.

3. Store in refrigerator for up to 10 days.

Avocado Cacao Mousse

(RAW, GLUTEN-FREE AND NUT-FREE)

Ingredients:

1 - 2 ripe avocados, skin and seed removed

1 - 2 ripe bananas, peeled

4 tablespoons raw cacao powder

2 tablespoons pure maple syrup

1 teaspoon vanilla extract

¼ teaspoon cinnamon, optional

½ cup water, plus more as needed

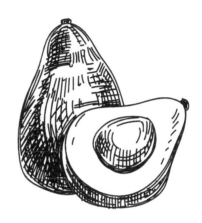

Method:

1. Mix all ingredients in a food processor until smooth and creamy.

2. Place in refrigerator for approximately ½ hour or until firm.

3. Garnish with **Vanilla Cashew Crème** (recipe can be found in this book) and fresh mint.

Avocado Key Lime Pie

By Dr. Ann Louise Gittleman

(RAW AND GLUTEN-FREE)

Ingredients:

2 tablespoons coconut butter

1 tablespoon coconut oil

1 cup pecans, chopped

½ cup unsweetened coconut flakes

½ teaspoon vanilla extract

1 pinch sea salt

2 ripe avocados

½ cup freshly squeezed lime juice
  (key limes are best, if you can get them)

⅓ cup monk fruit sweetener or date sugar

1 teaspoon lime zest

Method:

1. Melt coconut butter and coconut oil in a skillet over low heat.

2. In a food processor, pulse pecans and coconut flakes for 90 seconds.

3. Add the melted coconut butter and oil, vanilla and sea salt and process until the mixture sticks together, but retains a crumbly texture.

4. Press the mixture into the bottom and sides of a pie pan to form the crust.

5. Chill the crust in the refrigerator while making the filling.

6. Peel and pit the avocados and put them into a food processor or blender along with the lime juice, sweetener and lime zest.

7. Blend until smooth and thick.

8. Pour filling into the chilled crust and freeze for 3 hours or until center is firm.

9. Transfer to refrigerator and chill for 2 more hours before serving.

"G-Zen raised the bar and stands in a class all its own when it comes to vegan lifestyle eating. Chefs Mark Shadle and Ami Beach pour their hearts and souls into every tasty morsel. Together, they create food that is in harmony with the seasons and fresh and sustainable in every sense of the word. The recipes are delicious, nutritious and each one is more irresistible than the next. Kudos to this beautiful couple for making such an approachable plant-based book that anyone of any skill level can joyfully master and enjoy."

Ann Louise Gittleman, Ph.D., C.N.S.
New York Times award-winning author of 30 books on detox, health and healing

Baked Buffalo Cauliflower Bites

Ingredients:

1 cup soy milk or almond milk (unsweetened)

1 cup organic flour (any kind will work—even gluten-free!)

2 teaspoons garlic powder

1 head cauliflower, chopped into pieces

1 cup buffalo or hot sauce

1 tablespoon olive oil or melted vegan butter

Sea salt to taste

Paprika powder for garnish

Method:

1. Preheat the oven to 450°F.
2. Combine the soy milk or almond milk, flour and garlic powder in a bowl and stir until well combined.
3. Coat the cauliflower pieces with the flour mixture and place in a shallow baking dish. Bake for 18 minutes.
4. While the cauliflower is baking, combine the buffalo sauce and olive oil or vegan butter in a small bowl.
5. Pour the hot sauce mixture over the baked cauliflower and continue baking for an additional 5 to 8 minutes.
6. Plate cauliflower bites over a bed of romaine leaves, sprinkle with sea salt to taste and add paprika to garnish.

Serve with **Lemon Garlic Aioli** (recipe can be found in this book) and enjoy without the guilt.

This recipe can easily be made gluten-free by choosing a gluten-free flour.

These are great for parties or any entertaining and super quick and easy to make.

The Best Chocolate Icing Ever

By Dara Dubinet

(RAW, GLUTEN-FREE AND NUT-FREE)

Ingredients:

3 very ripe avocados

9 tablespoons cacao powder

5 tablespoons maple sugar or date sugar

3 tablespoons maple syrup

3 tablespoons coconut oil

2 - 3 drops liquid stevia

2 drops cinnamon oil, optional

2 pinches sea salt

Method:

1. Remove the skin and pit from the ripe avocados.
2. Add all ingredients to a high-speed blender and blend until creamy.
3. Taste and adjust flavor for sweetness, if desired.
4. Store in an airtight container for 5 to 7 days in the refrigerator.

Enjoy on fresh strawberries or anything that calls for a delicious and decadent, yet healthy, frosting.

Dara Dubinet is a Raw Foods Chef and Health Motivator of a clean, clear and bright lifestyle.
Check out **www.youtube.com/daradubinet** for inspirational videos and more info on her plant-based lifestyle.

Eat plant-based and live nine lives.

Blonde Macaroons Dipped in Chocolate

*G-ZEN FAVORITE
(RAW AND GLUTEN-FREE)

Ingredients: Macaroons

1 cup coconut butter, melted

2 cups shredded coconut

¾ cup maple syrup

1 teaspoon vanilla extract

½ teaspoon sea salt

Ingredients: Sauce

¾ cup maple syrup

⅔ cup raw cacao powder

⅓ cup coconut oil, melted

¾ teaspoon salt

¾ teaspoon vanilla extract

Method: Macaroons

1. In a food processor, mix all ingredients until well combined.

2. Use a melon baller to form balls.

3. Set aside while you make chocolate sauce.

Method: Sauce

1. In a food processor, mix all ingredients until smooth and creamy.

2. Dip macaroons halfway into chocolate sauce and place in refrigerator for 1 hour until firm.

3. Store in airtight container in the refrigerator or freezer.

Bombay Curried Veggie Burger with Avocado Coconut Spread

(GLUTEN-FREE)

Ingredients:

1 onion, finely chopped

2 garlic cloves, finely chopped

1 teaspoon ground coriander

1 teaspoon curry powder

1 can chickpeas (15 ounces), drained

1 - 2 handfuls walnuts or seeds, toasted in oil

1 - 2 large carrots, peeled and shredded

1 bunch fresh cilantro, chopped

1 lime, juiced

4 teaspoons coconut milk

1 "**Flax Egg**"
   (Recipe can be found in this book)

½ - 1 cup chickpea flour or gluten-free flour, as needed

1 - 2 teaspoons sea salt

1 pinch freshly ground pepper

2 tablespoons olive oil or coconut oil

Enjoy with a drizzle of vegan yogurt or **Avocado-Coconut Spread** and tomato on your favorite bread. Recipe for **Avocado-Coconut Spread** is on the adjoining page.

Method:

1. In a skillet, sizzle the onion and shredded carrots in heated oil until soft. Add the garlic, ground coriander and curry powder. Mix well. Cook for 1 - 2 minutes.

2. In a food processor, pulse the spiced onions and carrots, chickpeas, and nuts or seeds until well mixed (not pureed).

3. Place mixture into a bowl. Mix in fresh cilantro, lime juice, coconut milk and flax egg to bind.

4. Add salt and pepper to taste, and more curry powder, if you like an extra kick. If the burgers are too wet, add 2 - 4 tablespoons chickpea or gluten-free flour to help bind and hold the burger together.

5. Shape into patties, squeezing them firmly together. Dust your hands and the burgers with flour so they aren't too sticky.

6. Chill for at least 30 minutes, up to 2 hours, before cooking.

7. Sizzle burgers in a frying pan in a little oil (they're softer than meat burgers, so be careful if grilling). Cook until golden on both sides.

Avocado-Coconut Spread

Ingredients:

1 ripe avocado

3 teaspoons canned coconut milk

2 teaspoons lemon juice

1 teaspoon jalapeno, chopped and seeds removed

Salt and pepper, to taste

Method:

1. In a blender or food processor, mix all ingredients and spread on a veggie burger or use as a delicious dipping sauce.

2. Store in an airtight container in refrigerator for 5 to 7 days.

Burmese Zen Tofu

(GLUTEN-FREE AND NUT-FREE)

This recipe originated from the mountains of Burma. We love taking traditional recipes and making them work in a modern world.

Ingredients:

1 teaspoon coconut oil

1 cup chickpea flour

1 teaspoon salt, or to taste

1 teaspoon garlic powder

2 teaspoons nutritional yeast (optional)

¼ - ½ teaspoon turmeric powder

3 cups water, divided

The chickpea tofu is extra firm and can withstand pan frying or deep frying to make breaded cutlets. It is so versatile! The ways you can use this recipe are endless. **It will literally be a game changer in your kitchen.**

Method:

1. Grease an 8 x 8 baking dish with coconut oil.
2. In a medium bowl, mix together chickpea flour, salt, garlic powder, turmeric and nutritional yeast (optional).
3. Add 1 cup of water and whisk until smooth and creamy with no lumps.
4. Bring 2 cups of water to a boil over medium heat. Add the chickpea mixture and whisk, heating until the mixture is thick and glossy, 5 to 7 minutes.
5. Pour the smooth, thick mixture into the greased baking dish and cool to room temperature. Once the mixture is cool, refrigerate it, uncovered, for 1 hour.
6. To serve the tofu, upturn the baking dish and let the mixture slide out. Cut into strips or cubes and season and prepare the same way as you would any tofu recipe.
7. Store in airtight container for 5 to 7 days in the refrigerator.

It is soy-free, nut-free and gluten- free, yet is packed with protein and amino acids.

My peace prevail,
OM Shanti Om.

Butternut Squash, White Bean and Kale Ragout

(GLUTEN-FREE AND NUT-FREE)

Ingredients:

1 large (3 pounds) butternut squash

2 tablespoons coconut oil

2 tablespoons maple syrup

2 ½ teaspoons cider vinegar

1 teaspoon sea salt, or to taste

1 teaspoon ground black pepper

1 pinch cayenne pepper, or to taste

2 tablespoons extra-virgin olive oil

4 large leeks, white and light green parts only

4 large garlic cloves, minced
   (or use a garlic press)

2 teaspoons rosemary, fresh or dried

2 15-ounce cans cannellini beans,
   drained and rinsed

2 cups vegetable broth (or use vegan
   bouillon cubes and prepare according to instructions)

¾ pound kale, chopped (approximately 6 cups)

⅓ cup dried cranberries, chopped
   (plus additional berries for garnish)

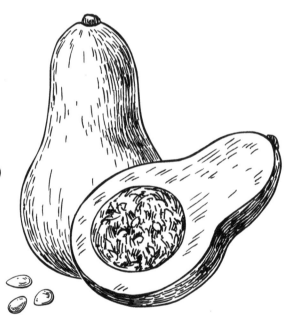

Method

1. Preheat oven to 425°F.
2. If using, dissolve vegan bouillon in hot water according to package instructions.
3. Peel squash, then halve squash and scoop out seeds. Cut flesh into 1-inch cubes.
4. Spread cubes out on a large rimmed baking sheet.
5. In a small saucepan, combine coconut oil, maple syrup, 1 teaspoon vinegar, salt, ½ teaspoon black pepper and cayenne pepper. Cook, stirring, over medium-high heat; pour mixture over squash and toss to coat evenly. Roast squash, tossing occasionally, until very tender and caramelized at edges, about 30 minutes.
6. In a large skillet, warm olive oil over medium heat. Add leeks, garlic, rosemary and a generous pinch of salt. Cook, stirring occasionally, until leeks are very soft and not at all browned, about 15 minutes.
7. Add beans and broth and simmer for 10 minutes.
8. Stir in kale. Simmer until kale is cooked down and very tender, about 10 to 15 minutes. Stir in squash and chopped cranberries; season with remaining 1½ teaspoons vinegar and ½ teaspoon black pepper.

Garnish with additional cranberries and a small pinch of sea salt. Serve.

Adapted from *New York Times* recipe. This stew is hearty, healthy and simply wonderful — a one-pot meal.

Recipe donated by Friends of Animals **www.friendsofanimals.org.**

An endorsement from Priscilla Feral
President of "Friends of Animals"

As a vegan, organic food activist in Connecticut and president of the non-profit animal advocacy group, Friends of Animals, I find G-Zen's restaurant in the shoreline town of Branford to be a refuge for sophisticated, abundant, artfully presented vegan cuisine at its best. Since the menu changes daily, selecting G-Zen's creations are always a delicious adventure that warms one's heart and soul.

Vegans and aspiring vegans will find friendship and support by either dining at Ami and Mark's restaurant, or preparing their nutritious, healthy and gorgeous recipes. At Friends of Animals, we're rooting for their continued success.

In Friends of Animals' Vegan Starter Guide, G-Zen is listed among our top 8 vegan restaurants across the country, and it's my personal favorite.

Priscilla Feral, President
www.friendsofanimals.org

Vegan is Love in Action

Cacao Coconut Snowflakes

*G-ZEN FAVORITE
(RAW, GLUTEN-FREE AND NUT-FREE)

Ingredients:

¼ cup raw coconut oil, liquefied

½ cup raw sesame tahini

½ cup maple syrup

1 cup coconut flakes

¼ cup raw cacao nibs

Handful of goji berries, optional

This is a fun, easy and quick recipe for the family to make year-round, but especially around the holidays. Try adding goji berries for more festive color around Christmas. Kids love making these, but adults love them just as much.

Method:

1. In a pan, liquefy the coconut oil, if necessary.
2. In a large mixing bowl, combine coconut oil, tahini and maple syrup. Mix well.
3. Add in the coconut flakes and cacao nibs according to desired taste. The more cacao nibs, the more energizing these will be. Please note, do not substitute shredded coconut for the coconut flakes, as it will not have the appearance of snowflakes.
4. Using a spoon, make 2- to 3-inch "snowflakes" and place on an oiled sheet pan or parchment paper.
5. Freeze for 15 to 30 minutes and serve.
6. Store in an airtight container in the freezer for up to 2 weeks.

Cacao and Coconut Truffles

*G-ZEN FAVORITE
(RAW, GLUTEN-FREE AND NUT-FREE)

Ingredients:

3 cups organic shredded coconut

1 ½ cups raw cacao powder

1 teaspoon Ceylon cinnamon powder

1 teaspoon lacuma powder (optional, but gives a rich carmel flavoring)

1 pinch Celtic sea salt

⅓ cup raw, cold-pressed coconut oil

¾ cup agave nectar, maple syrup or sweetener of choice

Method:

1. Combine all dry ingredients in a large mixing bowl and mix by hand, leaving about ¼ cup of shredded coconut on a separate plate for finishing touches.
2. In a small saucepan, slightly warm the coconut oil just enough to liquefy.
   Add coconut oil and sweeter to dry mix and mix well with a wooden spatula.
3. Use a teaspoon or melon baller and scoop out raw chocolate mixture into small balls.
   Slightly dampen hands and roll into round truffle-size pieces.
4. Finish by rolling each truffle in the shredded coconut. Dust each with a little Ceylon cinnamon for a final touch.
5. Put into refrigerator or freezer for 20 minutes and allow to harden.

When ready to serve, leave out for 10 minutes and serve with a sprig of fresh mint
and a dusting of cacao powder on the plate.

Caramel Date Pecan Superfood Ice Crème

(RAW AND GLUTEN-FREE)

Ingredients:

3 - 4 frozen bananas, cut into 1 - 2 inch pieces

1 tablespoon lacuma powder

1 teaspoon mesquite powder

1 - 2 vanilla pods, scraped or vanilla extract, to taste

½ cup dates, pitted and chopped

¼ cup organic pecans

2 tablespoons raw cacao nibs, optional

1 teaspoon toasted coconut flakes, optional

> Seriously, this is the easiest and tastiest guilt-free ice crème you will ever have.

Method:

1. Place bananas in a food processor fitted with an s-blade and add a tiny bit of water to help achieve the creamy texture of a soft-serve ice cream. This may take a little work. Continue to scrape down sides, slowly adding small amounts of water, as needed, to achieve creamy texture.
2. Mix in lucuma, mesquite and vanilla and process until well mixed.
3. Add chopped dates and pecans into the food processor and pulse a couple of times, leaving some chunky pieces, which adds texture and a nice presentation.
4. Fill your ice crème dish or parfait glass.

Top with chopped dates and one whole pecan, if desired. You can also sprinkle with cinnamon and garnish with a sprig of fresh mint! If you are feeling extra decadent, you can top with some **Vanilla Cashew Crème** (recipe can be found in this book), cacao nibs and toasted coconut flakes.

Cashew Parmesan Cheeze

(RAW AND GLUTEN-FREE)

Ingredients:

2 cups raw cashews

1 teaspoon sea salt, or to taste

2 tablespoons nutritional yeast, or to taste

Method:

1. In a food processor fitted with an s-blade, process all ingredients until a Parmesan cheese texture is achieved.
2. Store in the refrigerator and use as a vegan alternative to traditional Parmesan cheese.

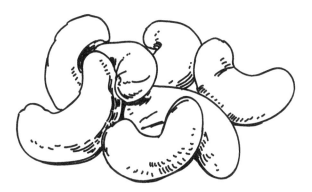

Cauliflower "Popcorn" Bites

(RAW, GLUTEN-FREE AND NUT-FREE)

Ingredients:

1 small head cauliflower

1 tablespoon lemon juice

1 tablespoon nutritional yeast

1 - 2 tablespoons extra-virgin olive oil or coconut oil (melted)

¼ teaspoon paprika (you can use smoked, too)

½ teaspoon Himalayan crystal salt or sea salt

2 large pinches turmeric

1 large pinch chili powder (or more, if you like it spicy)

5 drops pure liquid stevia or 1 teaspoon date paste, optional

2 tablespoons nutritional yeast for sprinkling, optional

Method:

1. Cut cauliflower into bite-sized pieces.
2. Combine lemon juice, nutritional yeast, olive oil, paprika, salt, turmeric, chili powder and stevia in a large mixing bowl. Stir well with a spoon.
3. Add the cauliflower pieces and stir again, making sure that every single piece is covered with the marinade.
4. Place the cauliflower pieces onto a dehydrator tray lined with a Teflex sheet. Sprinkle with the extra nutritional yeast to create a deep cheesy flavor.
5. Dehydrate at 115°F for 8 hours or longer, until the cauliflower is nice and crispy. Your "popcorn" is ready!

Cheezy Kale Chips

(RAW AND GLUTEN-FREE)

Ingredients:

2 bunches curly kale, de-stemmed

1 lemon, juiced

2 tablespoons sesame oil

½ cup sunflower seeds or pine nuts, finely ground

3 tablespoons nutritional yeast
   (or more, depending on taste)

1 tablespoon mesquite powder

Celtic sea salt, to taste

Method:

1. Wash and separate kale from hard stems and place in a large mixing bowl with lemon juice and sesame oil. Massage well.

2. Add ground nuts or seeds, nutritional yeast, mesquite powde, and salt, and toss until well coated.

3. Lay on dehydrator sheets or in a low temperature oven at 115°F until crisp.

Instead of potato chips, enjoy this healthy alternative. Kids and adults go wild for our cheezy, crunchy kale chips.

Chia Breakfast Pudding

by Dr. Ann Louise Glittleman

(RAW AND GLUTEN-FREE)

Ingredients:

½ cup chia seeds

1 ½ cups sesame, coconut or almond milk

½ teaspoon monk fruit or date sugar

¼ cup fresh berries, if desired

1 pinch sea salt

Method:

1. Stir all ingredients together.
2. Place in refrigerator and let sit 5 to 10 minutes to thicken. Then, stir every 15 minutes until the perfect consistency is reached and enjoy!

Ann Louise Gittleman, Ph.D., C.N.S.
New York Times award-winning author of 30 books on detox, health and healing

Zen Den by Chris Dyer

8 Beneficial Reasons to go Vegan

1) Prevent disease and support longevity: Meat eating has been linked to many types of cancer, heart disease, strokes, diabetes, hypertension, osteoporosis, kidney stones and many other devastating diseases. By eliminating meat and dairy products from your diet, you can take a crucial step towards a long life of health, happiness and ageless beauty.

2) Enjoy increased energy and endurance: A vegan diet improves your stamina, concentration and sense of well-being. In one scientific study, athletes who switched to a vegan diet improved their endurance almost 3 times as much as those who remained carnivores.

3) Avoid toxic food contaminants: Flesh foods are loaded with dangerous poisons and contaminants such as hormones, herbicides, pesticides and antibiotics. As these toxins are all fat-soluble, they are heavily concentrated in the fatty flesh of the animals. Not to mention the viruses, bacteria and parasites such as salmonella, trichinella spiralis and other worms and parasites found in meat and dairy products.

4) Care for the environment: By improperly using animals for food, we are eating ourselves off the planet. The raising of animals specifically to kill and consume them has resulted in incredible waste and devastation of our precious natural resources. Just one example of the consequences of the meat industry is the fact that, due to plundering our farmlands to fatten animals for slaughter, over 4 million acres of cropland are being lost to erosion in this country every year.

5) Help end world hunger: Every day, 40,000 children on this planet needlessly starve to death. According to the Department of Agriculture's statistics, one acre of land can grow 20,000 pounds of potatoes. That same acre of land, when used to grow cattle feed, can produce less than 165 pounds of edible meat products.

6) Become a more peaceful person: When we consume animal flesh products, we are at odds with nature and our fellow living beings. Consumption of plant-based foods naturally makes us more in tune with nature and our surroundings.

7) Veganism is moral and ethical: Given the devastating consequences of meat eating on an individual, social and ecological level, please consider the brilliant human beings before us that were advocates of a vegan lifestyle. Many great philosophers such as Plato, Socrates, Leo Tolstoy, Albert Einstein and George Bernard Shaw have taught the morality of veganism.

8) Understand how being vegan makes sense on every level of our existence. It feels good for us, for the environment and the animals.

Nothing tastes as good as Vegan feels

Classic Coconut Cupcakes

Dry Ingredients:

3½ cups whole-wheat pastry flour

½ tablespoon baking soda

1 tablespoon baking powder

1 tablespoon salt

1½ cups shredded coconut

Wet Ingredients:

½ box silken tofu

¾ cup vegetable oil

1 cup organic cane sugar or Florida Crystals®

1 tablespoon vanilla extract

½ teaspoon almond extract

1 can coconut milk

Method:

1. Sift all dry ingredients, except shredded coconut, and combine well.
2. In a food processor, process tofu until smooth, then add remaining wet ingredients to mix together.
3. Gradually add wet mixture to dry mixture without over mixing.
4. Fold in shredded coconut.
5. Pour batter into cupcake tins and bake at 300°F for 20 to 25 minutes.
6. Cool and frost.

Classic Vanilla Frosting with Coconut

Ingredients:

1 - 16-ounce container Earth Balance® butter substitute

¼ cup almond milk

3 cups confectioners' sugar

4 teaspoons vanilla extract

1 cup shredded coconut

Method:

1. Use a mixer with a paddle attachment and beat butter substitute until light and fluffy.

2. Add almond milk, sugar and vanilla and mix well. Then beat in coconut.

3. Let frosting firm up in refrigerator and then frost cupcakes.

> **Note:**
> In most cases, we would not use refined sugars in our recipes. But in this case, in order to achieve the texture of a classic cupcake and traditional frosting, we made an exception. We find this achieves the best frosting texture and, for those who can tolerate white sugar, we recommend that you follow the recipe as suggested.

Classic Cashew Crème Cheeze Spread

(RAW AND GLUTEN-FREE)

Ingredients:

1 cup raw cashews, soaked for at least 2 hours

¼ cup filtered water

¼ cup nutritional yeast

2 tablespoon lemon juice

2 garlic cloves

1 tablespoon raw apple cider vinegar

1 tablespoon Dijon mustard

Sea salt and fresh ground pepper, to taste

If you prefer the look of white crème cheeze, omit or lessen the amount of nutritional yeast.

Method:

1. Soak raw cashews in filtered water for at least 2 hours.
2. Simply add all ingredients into your Vitamix® or high-speed blender and blend until thick and creamy. (Mixture will be the consistency of thawed or stirred cream cheese and will further harden after being chilled.)
3. Store in the refrigerator for 5 to 7 days.

Enjoy!

The root of all joy is gratefulness.

Coconut Avocado Lime Soup with Sour Crème

(RAW AND GLUTEN-FREE)

Ingredients:

2 avocados

¾ medium cucumber

1 stalk celery

1 lime, juiced

Small handful of fresh coriander (cilantro)

2 teaspoons cumin

1 teaspoon ground coriander

½ teaspoon salt

1 teaspoon tamari

1 cup fresh Thai coconut water, or boxed
  if fresh coconut water is not available

Sour Crème (see recipe below)

Chives, chopped

Method:

1. Blend all ingredients, except the Sour Crème and chopped chives,
   in a high-speed blender until smooth.
2. Transfer to a serving bowl and garnish with Sour Crème and chopped chives.

Sour Crème

Ingredients:

1 ½ cups cashews

2 tablespoons lemon juice

1 tablespoon nutritional yeast

¾ teaspoon onion powder

1 teaspoon apple cider vinegar

1 cup water

½ teaspoon salt

Method:

1. Blend all ingredients in a
   high-speed blender.
   Add a little extra water,
   one tablespoon at a time,
   if needed.
2. Store in the refrigerator.

This is a versatile crème that can be used on soups, as a dip, or anywhere you would use traditional sour cream.

Coconut Ginger Cauliflower "Rice"

(GLUTEN-FREE AND NUT-FREE)

Ingredients:

1 head cauliflower, riced (about 5 cups)

1 cup yellow onion, diced

2 tablespoons coconut oil

1 tablespoon fresh garlic, minced

1 tablespoon fresh ginger root, grated

¼ teaspoon turmeric

¼ teaspoon paprika

¼ teaspoon salt

⅛ teaspoon black pepper

¼ cup coconut milk, canned and organic

1 tablespoon coconut aminos

2 - 3 limes

Coconut flakes and chopped mint or
    scallions, for garnish

Method:

1. Using a box grater, grate the florets off the cauliflower or pulse in a food processor until they reach a "rice-like" consistency. Be careful not to overprocess.
2. Combine the cauliflower, onion, coconut oil, ginger, garlic and all spices in a pan and sauté over medium heat for 10 minutes, until the cauliflower is soft and tender.
3. Add coconut milk and coconut aminos and simmer until the liquids have absorbed into the rice.
4. Juice one lime over the rice and garnish with lime wedges, coconut flakes and chopped mint or scallions.

Cauliflower coconut rice is a great way to enjoy all of the bursting flavors of coconut rice without the carbs. Try adding extras like fresh cilantro, mango and pineapple, to make an even more tropical version of this "no-rice," carb-friendly dish.

Coconut Raita

by Muneeza Ahmed

(GLUTEN-FREE AND NUT-FREE)

Ingredients:

1 can (16 oz) organic coconut milk

⅓ cup water

2 small lemons, juiced

1 teaspoon sea salt

1 teaspoon cumin

1 pinch cayenne pepper (or more, if you're brave)

½ cup cucumber, finely chopped

½ cup white onion, finely chopped

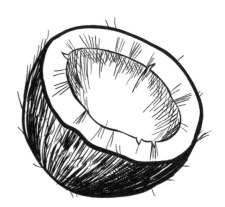

Method:

1. Empty the contents of the coconut milk can or box into a bowl and add the water and lemon juice. Blend well together to make a smooth liquid.
2. Add in the salt, spices and the veggies.
3. Mix well for an even distribution and place into the refrigerator.

Voila, your raita is ready.

Raita is a traditional favorite side/condiment from Pakistani cuisine. It is so versatile and delicious and can be used as a dipping sauce for breads, crackers and veggies.

Muneeza Ahmed, medical intuitive, energy healer, author, passionate food lover
www.muneezaahmed.com

Coconut and Zucchini French Toast

(RAW, GLUTEN-FREE AND NUT-FREE)

Ingredients:

2 cups golden flax meal

2 cups coconut flakes

¼ cup coconut water

2 - 3 ripe bananas

1 - 2 zucchini, peeled and chopped
   into small pieces

1 tablespoon vanilla extract

1 ½ tablespoons Ceylon cinnamon power

½ teaspoon lacuma powder

1 teaspoon maca powder

Method:

1. In a food processor, add flax meal and coconut flakes and process into a fine meal.
2. Add coconut water, bananas and zucchini pieces and process into a batter.
   If more water is needed to get the batter moving in the processor, add slowly.
3. Add vanilla, cinnamon, lacuma powder and maca powder and blend well.
4. Using parchment paper or standing dehydrator sheets, smooth the batter on with a
   spatula until you get the desired thickness of the toast.
5. Use a knife to score the size and shape of the French toast.
6. Place in dehydrator at 110°F for 6 hours, then gently flip toast.
7. Dehydrate for another 4-5 hours or until crisp on the outside and moist on the inside,
   similar to traditional French toast.

Serve warm with maple syrup and fresh fruit or **Vanilla Cashew Crème** (recipe can be found
in this book) with cinnamon dusted on top.

This recipe has literally made peoples' jaws drop! Adults and kids alike flip for this recipe. It's hard
to believe there is no flour, no sugar, no eggs, no baking and tastes so much like real French toast!

Please note: Depending on the climate or type of dehydrator, dehydration times may vary significantly.

Cornmeal Crusted Tempeh with Yellow Pepper Glaze

(GLUTEN-FREE AND NUT-FREE)

Ingredients: Tempeh

1 - 8-ounce package of tempeh

1 cup white wine

½ cup wheat-free tamari or nama shoyu

1 tablespoon garlic power

1 garlic clove, chopped

1 teaspoon dried basil

1 cup apple juice

2 cups non-GMO corn meal

½ cup extra-virgin olive oil

Ingredients: Yellow Pepper Glaze

4 cups yellow pepper, diced

1 cup maple syrup

1 cup brown rice vinegar

2 cups filtered water

1 tablespoon red and yellow pepper, diced for garnish

Method: Tempeh

1. Cut tempeh into 3 equal squares and slice each piece in half down the middle.
2. Combine wine, tamari, garlic powder, garlic, basil and apple juice to make a marinade.
3. Cover tempeh completely with marinade and let set in refrigerator for at least 4 hours.
4. Put cornmeal on a plate and cover both sides of tempeh.
5. Heat oil and sauté tempeh on both sides for 8 minutes or until golden brown.

Method: Yellow Pepper Glaze

1. Simmer peppers, maple syrup, vinegar and water for 20 minutes.
2. Puree with a hand blender and strain.
3. If it is too thin, cook longer to reduce the volume and increase thickness.

Serve warm, golden tempeh with the yellow pepper glaze on top and garnish with diced, fresh yellow and red peppers.

Country Style Mock Bacon

*G-ZEN FAVORITE
(GLUTEN-FREE AND NUT-FREE)

Ingredients:

1 - 8-ounce package organic tempeh, sliced into bacon-size strips

¼ cup tamari (wheat-free) or nama shoyu

2 teaspoons apple cider vinegar

1 teaspoon brown sugar

½ teaspoon ground cumin

½ teaspoon chili powder

½ cup water

2 teaspoons liquid smoke

1 teaspoon organic oil of your choice

1 pinch black or white pepper

Method:

1. Lay tempeh slices on a baking pan.
2. Bring tamari, vinegar, brown sugar, cumin, chili powder and water to a boil.
3. Stir in liquid smoke.
4. Pour mixture over tempeh slices, cover and chill for 2 hours.
5. Preheat oven to 300°F.
6. Line 2 baking sheets with parchment paper.
7. Place tempeh slices in a single layer on the lined baking sheets and brush with oil.
8. Bake for 10 to 15 minutes, flip over and bake another 7 minutes or until crisp.

This is one of our house favorites both at home for guests and on our G-Zen Buddha Brunch menu!

Creamy Chai Tea

by Dara Dubinet

(GLUTEN-FREE)

Ingredients:

5 cups spring water

5 tablespoons maple syrup or coconut sugar

4 tablespoons black tea (orange pekoe)

2 tablespoons cardamom pods, mottled

2 tablespoons cloves, mottled

2 tablespoons cinnamon bark, mottled

2 tablespoons star anise

1 large man thumb of ginger, sliced and mottled

1 teaspoon ground black pepper

2 ½ cups **Creamy Nut Milk** (see recipe below)

Method:

1. Add all ingredients, except nut milk, into a saucepan and slowly bring to a boil.
2. Stir the herbs around until they produce a "kick" in flavor.
3. Strain out the herbs, add the nut milk to the tea and bring heat up again to a low simmer.
4. Taste before serving and add anything additional if desired for flavor balancing.

Creamy Nut Milk

Blend 2 cups water with 1 cup nuts of choice. If using a fibrous nut like almonds, strain the mixture through a nut milk bag or cheesecloth before using. If you choose a high-fat nut like cashews, there is no need to strain. Use the homemade nut milk in place of commercial nut milk in any recipe.

Dara Dubinet is a raw foods chef and health motivator of a clean, clear and bright lifestyle.

Check out **www.youtube.com/daradubinet** for inspirational videos and more info on her plant-based lifestyle.

Creamy Tahini Dressing

(RAW, GLUTEN-FREE AND NUT-FREE)

Ingredients:

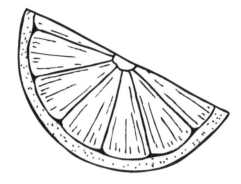

¾ cup raw tahini

½ - ¾ cup fresh lemon juice (about 4 lemons)

2 garlic cloves (or 1 teaspoon garlic powder)

¼ teaspoon onion powder

¼ teaspoon cumin powder

½ teaspoon sea salt

¼ cup water, or more for desired consistency

Method:

Combine all ingredients in a blender and blend until smooth and creamy.

Serve generously over your favorite veggies, or massage over raw kale for a perfect kale salad.

Crispy Onion Rings and Chipotle Mayo

(RAW AND GLUTEN- FREE)

Ingredients:

2 - 3 large onions

1 cup golden flax seeds, or
  ground flax meal

½ cup sunflower seeds

1 teaspoon paprika

1 teaspoon garlic powder

1 teaspoon sea salt, or to taste

¼ cup coconut oil, liquefied

¼ cup water

1 teaspoon tamari (gluten-free) or
  coconut aminos (soy-free)

1 - 2 teaspoons fresh-squeezed lemon juice or
  2 drops pure lemon essential oil

4 dates, pitted

1 pinch cayenne pepper

Method:

1. In a high-speed blender or Vitamix®, grind the flax seeds and sunflower seeds into a fine meal.

2. Add paprika, garlic powder, cayenne and sea salt. Mix well and set aside.

3. In a high-speed blender, mix coconut oil, water, tamari or coconut aminos, lemon juice or essential oil, dates and sea salt to taste. Blend on high for 3 minutes or until a creamy texture forms.

4. Slice the onions as thick as you wish (½ to 1 inch) and gently separate the slices into rings.

5. Dip each ring into the wet batter first. Then, dip them into the dry mixture and back again until well coated.

6. Place coated onions on a dehydrator mesh sheet or Teflex sheet and dehydrate them at 115°F until they are crisp. If you want to speed up the drying time, you can turn the temperature up to 135°F. Typically, it may take anywhere from 4 to 6 hours to get onion rings nice and crispy.

Serve with our **Chipotle Mayo** (recipe follows).

Chipotle Mayo

Ingredients:

¼ cup cashews

¼ cup sunflower seeds
   soaked 1 hour and drained

1 garlic clove

2 lemons, juiced

1 teaspoon of Bragg® Liquid Aminos

1 teaspoon umeboshi vinegar

1 pinch chipotle powder

Method:

1. Blend all the ingredients until you get a very smooth consistency.
2. Serve with onion rings or any sliced veggies.

Our crispy onion rings are absolutely addicting and total crowd pleasers no matter what the occasion. Experience for yourselves how good it feels to indulge in onion rings that are actually healthy for you.

Cucumber Zoodles with Mango Basil Dressing

by Rhia Cataldo

(RAW, GLUTEN-FREE AND NUT-FREE)

Ingredients:

3 large cucumbers (you can leave the skin on if they are organic, otherwise peel them)

2 ripe mangos, chopped

1 ½ cups fresh basil leaves

½ cup green onions

2 garlic cloves

1 orange, juiced

Sprinkle of thyme

2 cups cherry tomatoes

1 tablespoon hemp seeds

Tools needed: **spiralizer or julienne peeler and blender**

Method:

1. Spiralize/julienne cucumbers to make zoodles and set aside in a large bowl.
2. Blend together mango, basil, green onion, garlic, orange juice, and thyme.
3. Pour the dressing over the zoodles and mix together.
4. Top with cherry tomatoes and hemp seeds.
5. Refrigerate in an airtight container for 3 to 5 days to keep.

Thank your Angels and enjoy!

Rhia Cataldo Lifestyle
www.rhiacataldo.com

Curried Carrot Soup

by Rachel Feldman

(RAW, GLUTEN-FREE AND NUT-FREE)

Ingredients:

2 carrots, chopped

½ avocado

¾ cup water

1 teaspoon curry powder

¼ teaspoon coriander

⅛ teaspoon cumin

¼ teaspoon turmeric

⅛ teaspoon salt

1 tablespoon olive oil

1 tablespoon lime juice

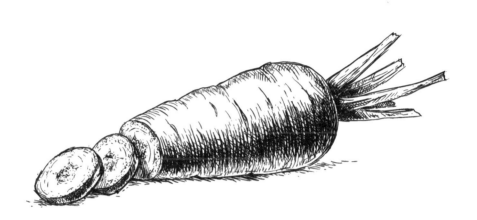

Method:

Place all ingredients in blender in order. Blend until smooth.

Serve as is or chill in the refrigerator for 30 minutes.

Rachel Feldman is a wellness momma, health coach and business niche coach. Today, Rachel teaches other health and wellness professionals the same system she used to build her successful health coaching practice. She's helped more than 8,000 health coaches rock their biz to the next level making the money they deserve.

Rachel Feldman, owner of rachelfeldman.com, health coach and business coach, contributor at Forbes, Huffington Post and Thrive Journal.

NOTHING WILL BENEFIT HUMAN
HEALTH AND INCREASE CHANCES OF
SURVIVAL FOR LIFE ON EARTH AS
MUCH AS THE EVOLUTION
TO A VEGAN DIET.

ALBERT EINSTEIN

Earth Candy Milkshake

(RAW, GLUTEN-FREE AND NUT-FREE)

Ingredients:

1/4 - 1/2 can coconut milk (canned only)

1/2 - 3/4 cup coconut water or filtered water, or as needed

1 cup frozen mango, unsweetened

1 teaspoon lacuma powder

1 teaspoon chaga powder

2 tablespoons maple syrup or to taste

3 - 4 tablespoons raw cacao nibs

1/2 -1 frozen banana (optional)

1 teaspoon coconut oil

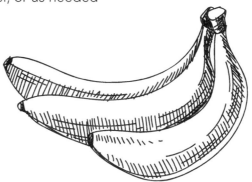

Method:

In a Vitamix® or high-speed blender, add all of the ingredients, slowly adding the coconut water or water to ensure the right texture of a thick milkshake. If it is too runny, add more frozen mango or banana. If the consistency is too thick, add a little more liquid.
Serve in a frosted pint glass and top with raw cacao nibs.

This is hands down one of the the healthiest and most decedent superfood milkshakes on the planet, but without the guilt.

Easy Creamy Tomato Sauce

by Dara Dubinet

(RAW AND GLUTEN-FREE)

Ingredients:

½ cup cherry tomatoes

1 tablespoon Meyer lemon juice or regular lemon juice

1 tablespoon plain Kite Hill® almond cream cheese style spread

  (or substitute 3 - 4 tablespoons cashews, soaked in water for 2 - 3 hours and drained)

1 tablespoon olive oil

¼ teaspoon garlic powder

2 pinches salt

1 pinch chili powder

1 - 2 medjool dates, if desired for sweetness

Method:

1. Combine all ingredients, except dates, in a high-speed blender and blend well. If making substitutions, i.e., regular tomatoes, it is best to taste mixture before serving to adjust flavor.
2. Sweeten with 1 to 2 medjool dates, pits removed, if you desire a little extra sweetness.

Enjoy this simple and delicious creamy tomato sauce over your noodle of choice whether it's a raw zucchini pasta or cooked gluten-free pasta.

Dara Dubinet is a raw foods chef and health motivator of a clean, clear and bright lifestyle.

Check out **www.youtube.com/daradubinet** for inspirational videos and more info on her plant-based lifestyle.

Peace beings on your plate.

Easy Mango Sorbet

by Mimi Kirk

(RAW, GLUTEN-FREE AND NUT-FREE)

Ingredients:

2 large ripe mangos

2 tablespoons agave or sweetener
  of choice, or to taste

1 lemon, juiced

Method:

1. Cut mango flesh from center pit.
2. Put all ingredients in a high-speed blender and blend until smooth.
3. Chill in a glass jar with lid in the refrigerator for 4 hours or overnight.
4. Once chilled, pour into a glass baking dish. (If you have an ice cream maker, follow manufacturer's directions.)
5. Freeze for 2 – 3 hours, after scraping with a fork so it doesn't freeze in one hard piece. Check the consistency after 2 hours. It could be ready to eat, or need a little more time in the freezer. Consistency is up to you.

It's that easy and so refreshing. Serve in a parfait dish with fresh mint.

Mimi Kirk, author, raw food chef, international speaker, and health and life coach. She is the author of *Live Raw, Live Raw Around the World*, and *The Ultimate Book of Modern Juicing*.

A Love Note from Mimi Kirk

I would do anything for Chefs Ami Beach and Mark Shadle. They are beautiful people. Everything they do is for the good of others. I've eaten their food and shared time with them and can't get enough of them or their delicious food. How many chefs do you know who grow much of their own food, feed their ducks by hand and take their food truck out with tasty vegan and raw food so more people can learn about healthy eating? And they do all this while keeping a great ethical restaurant and organic farm, in addition to operating the award-winning Gmonkey truck and several other green businesses. And I must also mention their consciousness about our planet and how they recycle and don't use chemicals to grow their food. They are really a model couple. That's some good folks, right?

Having food prepared with love is what they and their staff are all about. You can feel it in the atmosphere around them and in the dining experience itself. I've been to many raw and vegan restaurants around the world and G-Zen is tops in every way. They do everything for the right reasons and I'm honored to call them my friends.

I am ecstatic to have been asked to share a few of my vegan recipes and be a part of the G-Zen "Peace Begins on Your Plate" recipe book. After all, peace certainly does begin on our plate and how we feed and nurture our bodies has a huge impact on how we interact with the world. I am happy to join them in teaching the importance of a plant-based and vegan lifestyle and making it approachable to a larger audience.

Mimi Kirk, author, raw food chef, international speaker, and health and life coach. She is the author of *Live Raw, Live Raw Around the World,* and *The Ultimate Book of Modern Juicing*.

Easy Peasy Falafel Patties

(GLUTEN-FREE AND NUT-FREE)

Ingredients:

1 cup chickpea flour

½ teaspoon baking powder

½ - 1 teaspoon sea salt

1 teaspoon parsley flakes

1 teaspoon ground cumin

½ - 1 teaspoon ground coriander

½ - 1 teaspoon garlic powder

1 teaspoon minced onion

1 - 2 tablespoons fresh lemon juice

¼ - ½ cup warm water

Coconut oil or olive oil for frying

Method:

1. Combine all the dry ingredients in a large bowl and blend thoroughly.
2. Add the lemon juice and warm water and stir until well combined. Allow mixture to stand for 10 minutes.
3. In a heated and oiled skillet, using a teaspoon, add small amounts of batter and slightly flatten to create small patties. Depending on the size of the patties, you can do several batches.
4. Pan fry on each side for 5 to 7 minutes or until golden brown. Place on a piece of paper towel to absorb any excess oil from cooking.

This is a fool-proof, gluten-free version of traditional falafel. Not only is this tasty Middle Eastern dish completely gluten-free, but it is grain-free as well.

Serve on top of a salad, in a pita or on a bed of lettuce with tahini sauce or any dipping sauce of choice.

You can also try seasoning the patties with different ethnic flavorings, for example, Jamaican, Indian or anything you wish.

Easy Cashew Cheeze

(RAW AND GLUTEN-FREE)

Ingredients:

2 cups raw cashews or macadamia nuts
   (soaked in filtered water for 2 hours and drained)
¼ - ½ cup filtered water, as needed for
   desired consistency
¼ cup lemon juice, freshly squeezed
½ cup nutritional yeast
2 - 4 garlic cloves, minced
   (depending on preference)
1 teaspoon Celtic sea salt
1 teaspoon granulated garlic, optional
1 tablespoon fresh flat leaf parsley,
   chopped, optional

Ingredients Herbed Cheeze:

(For an herbed cheeze option, add
these additional ingredients along
with granulated garlic and parsley
from left.)
1 green onion, chopped
1 tablespoon fresh flat leaf parsley, chopped
1 tablespoon fresh basil, chopped
1 tablespoon fresh thyme, chopped
2 tablespoons nutritional yeast flakes
1 tablespoon fresh rosemary or sage

Method:

1. Place the cashews or macadamia nuts, ½ the water, ½ the lemon juice, nutritional yeast, garlic cloves and sea salt in a food processor and pulse until roughly blended.
2. Gradually add in more lemon juice and salt to taste.
3. Transfer the cheeze to a bowl and stir in the granulated garlic and parsley, if using.
4. Add more water for a creamier and thinner cheeze. Add less water for a thicker, more rustic cheeze.
5. Place in the refrigerator to set the cheeze for 30 minutes or until firm before serving.

The cheeze is best served after 24 hours in the refrigerator, but can be eaten sooner.
Store in airtight container in refrigerator for 7 to 10 days.

Epic Sunshine Seed Burger

(RAW, GLUTEN-FREE AND NUT-FREE)

Ingredients:

1 cup unsalted, raw sunflower seeds

1 cup raw pumpkins seeds

¼ cup hemp seeds

1 medium white onion, peeled and chopped

3 - 4 carrots, peeled and diced

¼ red pepper, seeded

1 zucchini (small or ½ medium) peeled and diced

3 - 4 dates, pitted

1 tablespoon fresh lemon juice

½ teaspoon curry powder

½ teaspoon turmeric powder

1 tablespoon coconut aminos

Salt and black pepper, to taste

1 dash paprika, optional

Method:

1. In a food processor fitted with an s-blade, add sunflower, pumpkin and hemp seeds and grind into small pieces or medium fine meal.

2. Add onions, carrots, pepper, zucchini, dates and lemon juice, using the pulse setting and mix thoroughly. It is helpful to add one ingredient at a time. Pulse until mixed thoroughly.

3. Add spices and coconut aminos and process for 1 to 2 minutes. If more liquid is needed, you can use more lemon juice or coconut aminos.

4. Season with salt, black pepper and paprika to taste.

5. Form large patties by hand or using a spatula and place onto baking sheets. Place in dehydrator at 115°F for 4 to 6 hours, turning after 2 hours to make sure the burgers are cooked through.

Serve as you would any burger with a tomato slice, lettuce, our **Simple Hemp Pesto** or **Smoked Ketchup** (recipes can be found in this book) on your choice of bread or salad. Enjoy this simple and delicious nut-free, soy-free and grain-free Sunshine Seed Burger.

Essential V-8 Immune Booster

(RAW, GLUTEN-FREE AND NUT-FREE)

Ingredients:

½ cup fresh basil

½ cup fresh cilantro

1 - 2 medium tomatoes

½ ripe avocado

2 garlic cloves

Handful of spinach

1 lemon, juiced

¼-inch piece raw ginger

½ - ¾ cup spring or filtered water,
   depending on consistency

½ - 1 teaspoon cayenne pepper

1 pinch dulse

1 pinch each Celtic sea salt and pepper, to taste

½ teaspoon horseradish, optional

This also makes a healthy alternative to a "Bloody Mary" cocktail with an organic alcohol of choice. Serve in a cocktail glass with a stick of celery and a fresh lemon wedge.

Method:

In a high-speed blender, mix all ingredients on high for 1 to 2 minutes.

Serve over ice with a lemon wedge and a basil leaf for garnish.

Everything Bagel

(RAW AND GLUTEN-FREE)

Ingredients:

1 cup almonds (soaked for at least 2 hours and drained)

1 cup carrots, peeled and diced

2 ½ tablespoons apple cider vinegar

¼ cup Bragg® Liquid Aminos

2 tablespoons olive oil

2 teaspoons sea salt

¼ cup flax seeds, ground

⅓ cup dehydrated onion powder (or minced onion flakes)

1 - 2 teaspoons garlic powder

1 - 2 tablespoons dry almonds, ground

¼ cup of sesame seeds, poppy seeds and
  onion flakes for garnish

The concept of a raw, gluten-free, grain-free bagel that you can easily make at home is revolutionary.

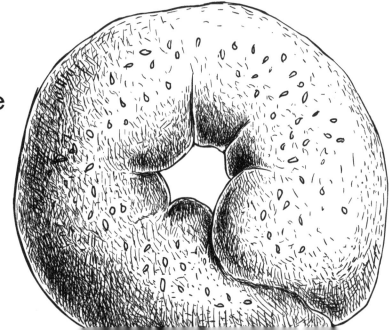

Method:

1. In a food processor, grind the soaked almonds and carrots together with the vinegar, liquid aminos, olive oil and sea salt.

2. Add the ground flax seeds, onion powder or flakes, and garlic powder and process until dough forms. You will need to keep scraping down the sides of your processor until it is well mixed. You may also need to add 1 to 2 teaspoons of water to get dough to the right consistency or set in refrigerator to firm up before forming.

3. With hands, form into rolls. Keep in mind that if you want to slice the bagel, it needs to be thick enough. It will shrink a little after dehydrating. Form the shape of a bagel with a hole in the middle using your finger.

4. Sprinkle the tops and sides with sesame seeds, poppy seeds and onion flakes, lightly pressing them in. Cover dehydrator trays with parchment paper or baking sheet, and use the ground almonds to dust the surface where you will be placing your bagels. This will also make them easier to flip.

5. Dehydrate at 105°F for about an hour or until the tops are slightly dry. Flip bagels over and sprinkle with more seeds, pressing them in.

6. Dehydrate another hour and flip back over.

7. Leave dehydrator on overnight or roughly 8 hours.

8. Carefully, with a sharp knife, slice bagels in half. Dry halves until desired texture, flipping periodically.

Serve with **Sunflower Seed and Herb Spread** or our **Classic Cashew Crème Cheeze Spread** (both recipes can be found in this book) or any cheese alternative.

Enjoy a little taste of heaven.

IT TAKES NOTHING AWAY FROM A HUMAN TO BE KIND TO AN ANIMAL.

Flax Egg, Egg Replacer

(RAW, GLUTEN-FREE AND NUT-FREE)

Ingredients:
1 tablespoon ground flax or chia seeds
3 tablespoons water

Method:
1. Whisk together the ground seeds and water until well combined.
2. Place in the refrigerator to set for 15 minutes.

Use as you would an egg in many of your favorite baking recipes.

Fresh Fruit Tart

(RAW, GLUTEN-FREE AND NUT-FREE)

Ingredients:

¾ cup raw pumpkin seeds, unsalted

1 cup tigernut flour

4 - 6 tablespoons raw cacao powder, optional (see note)

5 - 8 medjool dates, pitted and chopped, to taste

¼ teaspoon vanilla extract

1 pinch cinnamon

Fresh ripe fruit, diced

1 - 2 tablespoons water or coconut water, as needed

Note:

If you prefer a richer chocolate-tasting crust, follow the same recipe, but also add 4 to 6 tablespoons of raw cacao powder to the ingredients. If you add cacao powder, you may need to add slightly more water to get the dough to form. Feel free to adjust the amount of cacao or dates to get the right taste and balance of flavors.

** Tigernut flour is not a nut, but actually a tuber, a small root vegetable. Tigernut is the #1 source of resistant starch, a prebiotic fiber that resists digestion and becomes fuel for our probiotic bacteria. Tigernut is gluten-free, nut-free and Paleo friendly and has been used by ancient cultures for thousands of years.

Method:

1. In a food processor fitted with an s-blade, add pumpkin seeds and tigernut flour and process into a fine meal. If using the cacao option, add it now using the pulse setting on the food processor, and combine well.

2. Add pitted and chopped dates, vanilla extract and dash of cinnamon. Using the pulse setting, slowly add 2 to 4 tablespoons of filtered water or coconut water and pulse well until you see a ball of dough form and it is well mixed.

3. Remove dough from food processor and press into small 4-inch tart dishes (purchase online or in any kitchen supply store).

4. Place in dehydrator at 115°F for 3 to 4 hours or until golden brown.

5. Use fresh, organic raspberries, strawberries and mango slices and place on top of tart in center.

Top with **Vanilla Cashew Crème** (recipe can be found in this book) and fresh mint and serve warm.

Fresh Mango Country Cobbler

(RAW AND GLUTEN-FREE)

Ingredients:

3 cups pecans

1 vanilla bean, scraped

1 teaspoon cinnamon powder

¼ teaspoon sea salt

¾ cup pitted dates

6 cups ripe mango, diced (3 - 4 ripe, organic mangos)

¾ cup dates

3 tablespoons raw coconut oil

½ cup filtered water or coconut water (or as needed)

Method:

1. In food processor, mix pecans, vanilla bean, cinnamon and salt until you get a fine powder.
2. Add pitted dates, one at a time, until well mixed.
3. Sprinkle half the mixture into a glass pie dish for the crust and set other half aside for topping.
4. In food processor, mix dates, coconut oil and coconut water as needed until a thick syrup consistency is reached and set the syrup aside.
5. Place mango into a large mixing bowl and toss with syrup until well coated.
6. Add mango mixture on top of the crust in the pie plate and top with remaining crust crumble.

Serve with **Vanilla Cashew Crème** (recipe can be found in this book) and a few fresh mango slices and cinnamon.

Garlic Lemon Aioli

(RAW AND GLUTEN-FREE)

Ingredients:

1 cup raw cashews, soaked for a least 3 hours and drained

¼ cup filtered water

1 garlic clove, chopped

¼ cup fresh lemon juice

½ teaspoon powdered garlic

1 ¼ teaspoons mustard

1 teaspoon apple cider vinegar

¼ teaspoon tahini

¼ teaspoon sea salt

Method:

Add all ingredients into a food processor and mix until creamy.

Add the aioli to the top of our **Raw Falafel** (recipe can be found in this book) and serve over a bed of lettuce garnished with a lemon wedge. Also makes a great dipping sauce for veggies, appetizers or as a dressing for kelp noodles.

G-Glo Beauty Juice

*G-ZEN FAVORITE
(RAW, GLUTEN-FREE AND NUT-FREE)

Ingredients:

½ beet, peeled

½ bunch spinach

3 stalks celery

1 apples

1 cucumber

1 leaf green kale

1-inch piece ginger root

1 lime

1 lemon

Method:

Use a high-speed juicer and juice away. If using organic ingredients, feel free to juice the lemon, apple and lime with the peel for maximum nutrients. Add more apple or ginger according to your taste.

Juice it up and enjoy!

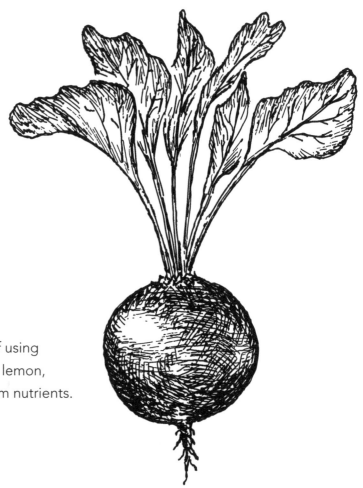

Glow Beauty Blended Green Soup

(RAW, GLUTEN-FREE AND NUT-FREE)

Ingredients:

2 large handfuls baby spinach

1 handful fresh cilantro

1 - 16 oz package cherry tomatoes

2 cloves raw garlic, peeled

½ cup fresh pineapple, diced (optional)

1 teaspoon dulse flakes (optional)

1 lemon, halved

2 oranges, halved

Method:

1. In a Vitamix®, add all of the ingredients except for the lemon and oranges.
2. With a hand-held citrus juicer, juice the lemon and oranges and add the juice into the blender along with other ingredients.
3. Set blender on high and while using the Vitamix® tamper tool, press down until all ingredients are well combined. You should have a smooth green soup texture.

Serve in a bowl, we prefer a wooden bowl, and garnish with chopped cilantro.

This Glow Beauty Blended soup is a perfect go-to any time you want to have a detoxifying meal, reboot your digestion or add more vitality to your day. For a mini-detox, you can enjoy this soup for breakfast and lunch and have a raw meal for dinner. This is a perfect one-day detox that will do wonders for your body and soul.

Inhale love. Exhale gratitude.

Golden Mandala

(RAW, GLUTEN-FREE AND NUT-FREE)

Ingredients:

3 oranges, peeled

6 - 8 carrots

2-inch piece fresh turmeric root

1-inch piece fresh ginger root, or more to taste

1-inch piece burdock root

1 lime

1 lemon

1 apple

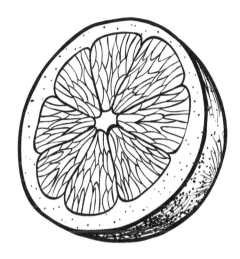

Method:

With a high-speed juicer, juice all of the above ingredients. If using all organic ingredients, all the skins can be juiced for optimal nutrients, with the exception of the oranges.

This elixir is amazing for inflammation, digestive health and the immune system.

Greek-Style Spanakopita

*G-ZEN FAVORITE
(NUT-FREE)

Ingredients:

1 - 2 tablespoons olive oil

1 tablespoon garlic, minced

2 - 10-ounce bags spinach

2 - 12-ounce blocks tofu, pressed

2 teaspoons dried oregano

2 teaspoons dried basil

1 tablespoon nutritional yeast

1 teaspoon nutmeg

Salt and pepper, to taste

1 package frozen whole-wheat phyllo sheets
   (approximately 12 - 14 sheets)

½ - 1 cup light olive oil

Topping:

1 tablespoon salt

1 tablespoon black pepper

1 tablespoon turmeric

1 tablespoon paprika

Method:

1. Pre-heat oven to 400°F.
2. Heat 1 to 2 tablespoons olive oil in a skillet. Sauté garlic and wilt spinach.
   Stir often and remove from heat as soon as spinach is wilted and garlic is fragrant.
3. Strain and remove excess liquid, let cool.
4. In a food processor, place tofu, herbs, nutritional yeast, nutmeg, salt and pepper and mix well.
5. Add spinach and mix again.
6. Lay out a phyllo sheet and brush with light olive oil using a pastry brush.
7. Add another sheet so you have two layers and brush with oil.
8. Place a finger-sized strip of filling at base, roll like a cigar and place on oiled sheet pan.
9. Cut roll into 1-inch pieces with a serrated knife.
10. Mix spices together for the topping and lightly sprinkle on top.
11. Bake at 400°F for 8 minutes or until golden brown.

This is one of our famous appetizers both at the restaurant and for catering.

Enjoy!

DON'T BE EYE CANDY,
BE SOUL FOOD.

Green and Black Chocolate Maca Banana Kale Chips

(RAW AND GLUTEN-FREE)

Ingredients:

1 bunch kale (curly kale works best)

1 cup banana, chopped

½ cup nut milk (hempseed milk will work too)

¼ cup cold-pressed coconut oil, warmed to liquefy

⅓ cup cacao powder

1 teaspoon vanilla extract

½ teaspoon sea salt

¼ cup maple syrup

1 teaspoon maca powder

1 teaspoon lacuma powder

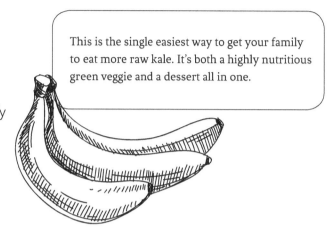

This is the single easiest way to get your family to eat more raw kale. It's both a highly nutritious green veggie and a dessert all in one.

Method:

1. Remove stems from kale leaves and chop the leaves into bite-sized pieces.
2. Wash kale pieces and dry.
3. Place the rest of the ingredients into a blender and blend to a creamy smooth texture.
4. In a bowl, pour mixture over kale pieces and thoroughly mix with hands until each piece is coated with the chocolate mixture.
5. Place the coated kale onto food dehydrator trays (or cooking trays if using the oven) and dehydrate at 115°F for 6 to 8 hours, until desired crunchiness is achieved. If you do not have a dehydrator, bake at 300°F for 20 minutes. Flip, and bake for another 10 minutes or so. You can also bake at 200°F with the oven door ajar. It will take longer, but the results will be closer to that of a dehydrator.

Green Goddess Dressing

by Muneeza Ahmed

(RAW, GLUTEN-FREE AND NUT-FREE)

Ingredients:

1 avocado

½ bunch cilantro

½ bunch parley

4 sprigs mint

1 teaspoon coconut oil (or use ½ cup coconut water
to keep low-fat)

1 lemon

½ cup coconut water

¼ cup hemp seeds

¼ cup pumpkin seeds

Salt, to taste

Method:

In a high-speed blender, mix all ingredients together
and blend until smooth and creamy.

Muneeza Ahmed, medical intuitive, energy healer, author, passionate food lover

www.muneezaahmed.com

Green Monkey Smoothie

(RAW AND GLUTEN-FREE)

Ingredients:

½ cup apple juice (organic and fresh pressed is best)

½ cup nut milk, almond or coconut is our favorite

½ -1 cup filtered water

5 kale leaves, stems removed

¾ cup parsley tops

½ cup cashews

1 - 2 teaspoons fresh lime juice

2 slices fresh ginger

3 - 4 dried black figs

½ cup organic hempseed

2 - 3 tablespoons organic extra-virgin coconut oil

1 ripe banana

1 cup ice

Method:

In a high-speed blender or preferably a Vitamix®, combine all ingredients together and blend until smooth and creamy.

This green smoothie makes a great meal replacement that will super-power you through your day. It's packed full of vitamins, minerals and omega fatty acids and is super delicious and satisfying.

Guilt-Free Pasta and Sundried Tomato Marinara

*G-ZEN FAVORITE
(RAW AND GLUTEN-FREE)

Ingredients: Noodles

3 medium zucchini

3 large carrots

3 medium beets

Ingredients: Marinara

2 cups sundried tomatoes in oil

2 cups tomatoes, diced or chopped

2 cups cashews (soaked at least 1 hour and drained)

1 cup of medjool dates, pitted

1 teaspoon oregano

1 teaspoon rosemary

1 cup basil

2 garlic cloves

1 pinch black pepper, or to taste

1 pinch Celtic sea salt, or to taste

Chili pepper flakes, optional

Ingredients: Cashew Parmesan Cheeze

2 cups dried cashews (soaked 1 hour and drained)

1 teaspoon Celtic sea salt

1 tablespoon nutritional yeast

This is one of our most popular raw-inspired dishes at the restaurant!

Method:

1. Using a spiralizer, cut long noodle-like pieces from the beets, carrots and zucchini. You can also use a vegetable peeler or shredder attachment to a food processor to make shorter vegetable noodles. Set noodles aside.
2. Combine all of the marinara ingredients in a food processor fitted with an s-blade. Pulse until you get a creamy marinara. Remove and set aside.
3. For the Cashew Parmesan Cheeze, place the raw cashews, Celtic sea salt and nutritional yeast into a food processor fitted with an s-blade until a Parmesan cheese texture is reached.
4. In a large mixing bowl, combine all vegetable noodles and sundried marinara and toss until the vegetable pasta is well covered with sauce.

Serve on a plate and top with plenty of Cashew Parmesan Cheeze to add a rich and cheesy flavor. Garnish plate with fresh chopped herbs, basil and dried oregano.

Voila, a raw, guiltless version of pasta and Italian marinara.

It's gluten-free and Paleo friendly, too!

About Mark Shadle

Chef Mark Shadle, a vegetarian for more than 30 years, grew up in a traditional meat-eating family and spent time in rural Pennsylvania on his family's farm haying, planting the garden and learning all that he could from the farm experience. "I saw it all first hand," he says. "There was a great respect for the food and the land." Mark's deep reverence for farming and foods stayed with him his whole life and became his life's passion and mission. Mark is largely self-taught, but credits his late mother, Carol Shadle, for his interest in slow foods and sourcing ingredients locally. He takes great inspiration from his favorite reference, "The Natural Cuisine of Georges Blanc," a gorgeously illustrated compilation of food artistry based on the acclaimed restaurant in the Burgundy region of France. The spirit of this can be found in many of his elegant and flavorful recipes.

Over the more than two decades of his culinary career, Mark has made a tremendous impact on the local, sustainable and natural foods movement. As a member of the American Natural Foods team, his team garnered two Gold, one Silver and one Bronze medal in the Culinary Olympics in Germany. As a vegetarian team battling 60 countries and all genres of food, Mark brought home two Gold medals for the USA, which was a defining moment in his culinary career.

Chef Mark had the high honor of being invited to the White House by First Lady Michelle Obama and is currently involved with the "Chefs Move to School" initiative that involves working directly with schools and helping to bring awareness to healthier food choices for children. Executive Chef Mark is one of the most celebrated vegan chefs working today and a pioneer of organic, environmentally conscious cuisine both locally and internationally.

The concept of Farm to Table, in its purist sense, conjures images of wholesome food being plucked right from the garden and served directly to the table. But Chef Shadle is bringing added value to this recent hot trend in food culture by focusing on the vital importance of preserving small organic Connecticut farmlands and growing his own nutritious food. Shadle Farm, in historic Durham, CT, has become one of the organic suppliers for his very own G-Zen restaurant in Branford, CT.

"Seed to Table" is his motto, growing many of the organic ingredients on the farm himself and then serving them at the restaurant, taking the concept to a whole new level.

Throughout his culinary career, Mark's extensive knowledge of vegetarian/vegan cooking, hands-on experience and deep respect for nature has cultivated his approach to holistic cuisine in a way that is distinctly his own. You simply can taste the love in everything he cooks.

Under Chef Mark's culinary reigns, G-Zen has quickly become a mecca for vegetarians and vegans on the East coast and beyond. He proudly represents Connecticut and continues to create some of the most innovative, healthy and creative plant-based foods on the planet.

He is ecstatic to be the Executive Chef of the award-winning G-Zen culinary team and plans on expanding the "G" brand with more green enterprises in the near future.

When Chef Mark is not cooking at G-Zen or on the Gmonkey mobile food truck, he is found working on his sustainable farm in Durham, CT, planting tropical fruit trees in the Caribbean at his second home in Culebra, PR, tending to his bees or lecturing about a sustainable lifestyle.

In addition, Chef Mark has had the honor of serving his conscious cuisine to many celebrities over the years including amazing people like the rock legend *Neil Young & Crazy Horse, Billy Joel, Chrissie Hynde, Danny DeVito, Moby, Kevin Costner and LA's Chef Tal Ronnen,* to name just a few.

A TRANQUIL WAY
TO QUIET THE MIND
Lies IN NATURE.

Mark Shadle

G-Zen House Botanical Sake Mojito

(RAW, GLUTEN-FREE AND NUT-FREE)

Ingredients:

1 quart fresh pineapple juice from 5 - 6 pineapples
(or store bought, cold pressed in glass jar
by Lakewood)

1 quart fresh-pressed apple juice from 6 - 8 apples
(or store bought, cold pressed in glass jar
by Lakewood)

1 quart fresh Thai coconut water
(or store-bought, preferably organic and not
from concentrate)

1 handful fresh basil leaves

1 handful fresh spearmint

1 handful fresh peppermint or lemongrass

2 - 3 drops white grapefruit essential oil

2 - 3 drops blood orange essential oil

1 - 2 drops lemon essential oil

1 - 2 drops lime essential oil

3 - 4 cups unfiltered sake, or to taste

¼ cup raw agave, maple syrup or
liquid sweetener

Method:

1. Juice pineapple and apples, like we do at G-Zen,
   or use store-bought juices and pour into a pitcher.
2. Add the coconut water, fresh mint, basil and essential oils.
3. Muddle the basil and mint to release the flavors and aromas.
4. Add liquid sweetener to taste.
5. Refrigerate the mixture overnight in a glass container or pitcher.

Serve over ice with fresh mint and basil leaves.

People wait all year for our seasonal harvest of fresh basil, various mints and herbs at our farm, "Shadle Farm." We love making our seasonal botanical mojitos and craft cocktails.

Healing Kitchari Recipe

(GLUTEN-FREE AND NUT-FREE)

Ingredients:

2 cups yellow mung bean dal

2 tablespoons sesame or coconut oil

2 teaspoons each black mustard seeds, cumin
seeds, turmeric powder, and black pepper

2 bay leaves

1 teaspoon each cumin powder,
coriander powder, fennel seeds

1 cup white basmati rice

8 cups water

2 cloves

2 - 5 cups organic, seasonal vegetables
such as spinach, carrots, celery, kale and
bok choy, chopped

1 cup fresh cilantro, chopped, optional

Method:

1. Rinse the mung dal beans and strain them five times, or until the water runs clear.
2. Heat the oil in a large pot. Add all the seeds and toast until the mustard seeds pop.
   Add the bay leaves and powdered spices, and mix together.
3. Stir in the rice and mung dal beans. Add 8 cups of water, cloves and chopped vegetables.
4. Bring to a boil and reduce to a simmer.
5. Cook at least one hour, until the beans and rice are soft and the kitchari has a
   porridge-like consistency.

Serve warm with fresh cilantro on top, if desired.

Kitchari has been made in India for thousands of years. It is traditionally made of yellow mung bean dal and basmati rice, along with digestive spices and oil. It is used as a cleansing and detoxifying food in Ayurveda and is powerful and restorative to the body. Kitchari is very nourishing, especially in fall and winter, and can be used as part of a cleansing diet or as a satisfying mono-meal.

Herbed Nut Burgers

(RAW AND GLUTEN-FREE)

Ingredients:

4 large carrots, peeled

1 medium onion or bunch of scallions

1 small zucchini, peeled

2 cups almonds or Brazil nuts

2 cups pecans

¼ cup flax meal

1 handful fresh parsley

1 handful fresh basil, or 1 teaspoon dried

¼ cup lemon juice, or more depending on consistency

1½ teaspoons salt

3 teaspoons dried rosemary

1 teaspoon dried sage

2 teaspoons curry powder

½ cup sundried tomatoes (soaked until soft and drained)

1 teaspoon coconut aminos, or to taste

Method:

1. Roughly chop carrots, onions and zucchini.
2. Add all ingredients to a food processor and process until finely chopped and well mixed.
3. Shape into burgers by hand. Dehydrate for 5 to 6 hours at 125°F, turning burgers once after about 2 hours.
4. Store in an airtight container for 5 days in the refrigerator.

Serve in place of any cooked veggie burger, on top of a salad or on raw bread. Top with our **Smoked Ketchup** and **Simple and Quick Hemp Pesto** (recipes can be found in this book) for added flavor. The burger is grain-free, gluten-free and so easy and delicious.

Hold the Chickpea Hummus

(RAW, GLUTEN-FREE AND NUT-FREE)

Ingredients:

2 zucchini, peeled and chopped (about 2 cups)

1 avocado

½ cup raw tahini

¼ cup fresh lemon juice

½ teaspoon coconut aminos, optional

2 tablespoons olive oil

½-inch piece fresh ginger

½ garlic clove

½ teaspoon salt

1 pinch cayenne pepper, optional

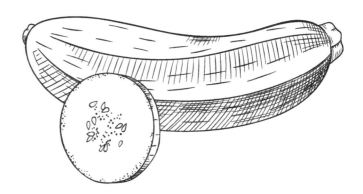

Method:

1. Place all the ingredients in a food processor and process until smooth.

2. Stop occasionally to scrape down the sides of the bowl with a rubber spatula.

3. Store in the refrigerator in an airtight container for up to 4 days.

This is great on a wrap, crackers or a salad! This recipe is also Paleo friendly and low in carbs and sugar.

Hold the Mayo "Nayonaise"

*G-ZEN FAVORITE
(GLUTEN-FREE AND NUT-FREE)

Ingredients: Noodles

2 - 12-ounce boxes silken tofu

½ teaspoon sea salt

½ teaspoon pepper

¼ teaspoon turmeric

¼ teaspoon paprika

¼ cup fresh lemon juice

¼ cup apple cider vinegar

2 tablespoons maple syrup

1 cup extra-virgin olive oil

Method:

1. In a food processor, add all ingredients, except for the oil, and mix until smooth and creamy.

2. Slowly add oil in a steady stream to create emulsified nayonaise.

3. Store in an airtight container in refrigerator for 5 to 7 days and use in place of traditional mayonnaise without the guilt.

Hot Chocolate Elixir

by Gabriellle Brick

(GLUTEN-FREE AND NUT-FREE)

Ingredients:

½ cup organic coconut milk

1 ounce organic cacao paste or
   3 tablespoons organic cacao powder

¼ teaspoon organic turmeric powder
   (or turmeric extract powder)

1 teaspoon organic maple sugar

1 pinch Celtic sea salt

Method:

1. Gently warm the coconut milk and pour into a blender.
2. Add the rest of the ingredients and blend.

Pour into your favorite mug and enjoy.

Gabrielle Brick
virtual business partner – green product development – lifestyle design
www.gabriellebrick.com

House Vegetable Dumplings and Ginger Tamari Dipping Sauce

*G-ZEN FAVORITE
(NUT-FREE)

Ingredients: Filling

2 - 3 tablespoons toasted sesame oil

1 cup carrots, shredded

1 cup mushrooms, shredded

1 cup scallions, chopped

1 tablespoon fresh garlic, minced

Salt and pepper, to taste

1 tablespoon fresh ginger, minced

1 - 1.3-ounce package cellophane
   rice noodle, vermicelli style

Ingredients: Dumplings

1 - 16-ounce package dumpling wraps

½ cup cornstarch (non-GMO)

1 cup water

Method:

1. Sauté vegetables in sesame oil with garlic, salt and pepper. Remove from heat and place in another pan to cool.

2. Soak noodles in a bowl of warm water for 10 minutes to allow them to expand, then strain and rough chop noodles into small sections.

3. In a food processor, mix the rest of the filling ingredients, including the noodles, until you coarse, yet smooth, filling texture.

4. Lay out 4 dumpling wraps. Mix cornstarch and water together and then put a spoonful of liquid around the outside rim of each wrapper.

5. Put one heaping teaspoon of filling into the center of each dumpling wrap. Fold up and fork edges to create a finished look for the dumpling.

6. Drop into simmering water for 5 minutes, remove with a strainer and serve with **Ginger Tamari Dipping Sauce** (recipe next page).

You will find this delicious dumpling on our Dim Sum Platter, one of the most popular appetizers at G-Zen, along with the Ginger Tamari Dipping Sauce.

Ginger Tamari Dipping Sauce

Ingredients

1 tablespoon fresh garlic, minced

1 tablespoon fresh ginger, minced

2 tablespoons scallions, chopped

1 cup tamari

½ cup apple cider vinegar

½ cup white wine

2 cups water

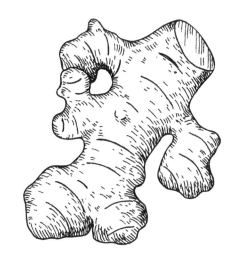

Method:

Mix all ingredients together in a bowl and serve in small dipping bowls.

Voila! Makes a perfect dipping sauce for vegetable dumplings or any vegetarian sushi roll or wrap.

Kale Salad with Ginger Almond Butter Sauce

by Medical Medium

(RAW AND GLUTEN-FREE)

Ingredients:

2 tablespoons almond butter

½ cup water

1 date

1 garlic clove

1 quarter-sized slice of ginger

½ lemon, juiced

¼ cup cilantro

2 heads kale

1 cup cabbage, finely shredded

4 green onion stems, chopped

2 tablespoons sunflower seeds

Method:

1. To make the almond butter sauce, blend almond butter, water, date, garlic, ginger, lemon juice and cilantro until smooth.
2. Remove stems from kale and finely chop the leaves.
3. Place kale into a large bowl. Massage dressing into the kale until kale softens and reduces.
4. Toss with cabbage, green onion and sunflower seeds.
5. Store in the refrigerator for up to 3 days.

This kale salad is hearty and full of flavor. It only gets better the next day, so make a double batch and keep half in the refrigerator for an on-the-go lunch! Don't be afraid to get your hands in there and really massage that kale. You'll be amazed how tender and delicious it becomes.

From Anthony William, *New York Times* best-selling author of Medical Medium:
Secrets Behind Chronic Illness and How To Finally Heal
www.MedicalMedium.com

Lavender Lemonade

(GLUTEN-FREE AND NUT-FREE)

Ingredients:

2 cups water

½ cup coconut sugar

¼ cup agave nectar or maple syrup

3 tablespoons dried lavender

2 cups freshly squeezed lemon juice

4 cups water

1 lemon, sliced, for garnish

Method:

1. Over medium heat, combine water and sugar, bringing to a boil until sugar is dissolved.
2. Remove from heat and stir in agave nectar or maple syrup and dried lavender. Cover for about 15 minutes, allowing mixture to steep.
3. Strain lavender, making sure to release all juices and syrup.
4. In a large pitcher, combine freshly squeezed lemon juice, lavender mixture and water.
5. Chill for at least 2 hours.

Enjoy over ice!

This refreshing special is regularly served at G-Zen during the summer months.

Lemon Coconut Snowballs

(RAW, GLUTEN-FREE AND NUT-FREE)

Ingredients:

1 cup virgin coconut oil, warmed slightly to liquefy

4 - 6 tablespoons coconut nectar or sweetener of choice, to taste

1 pinch sea salt

1 ½ cups unsweetened, shredded coconut

1 teaspoon vanilla extract

1 ½ cups hemp seeds

4 - 6 drops lemon essential oil

Method:

1. In a large bowl, mix all ingredients, except ½ cup of hemp seeds saved for garnishing.
2. Form into 1-inch balls. If the mixture is too wet to form balls, add more shredded coconut or hemp seeds.
3. Roll into uniform shaped balls and roll half of them into hemp seeds. The other half can be left as is or you can be creative and roll them in more coconut or cacao nibs.
4. Place on a plate and chill in freezer.
5. Store in an airtight container in freezer for up to 1 month.

Serve cold.

During the holidays, you can use beet juice or spirulina to color the shredded coconut to make a more festive snowball. You can also substitute the lemon essential oil with peppermint or any other flavor. This recipe is so easy and delicious, yet can be made and ready to serve in less than 10 minutes, which makes this a go-to recipe for our friends and family.

Live the life you love, love the life you live.
Bob Marley

Lemon Drop Tart

*G-ZEN FAVORITE
(GLUTEN-FREE)

Ingredients: Lemon Goo

3 cups raw cashews

6 tablespoons agar-agar flakes

1 ½ cups maple syrup

⅓ teaspoon sea salt

2 cups lemon juice

2 tablespoons vanilla

4 cups rice milk

Zest of 5 lemons

Ingredients: Tart Crust

2 ½ cups raw almonds

½ cup coconut oil

½ cup rolled oats (gluten-free)

¼ cup maple syrup

Ingredients: Tart

2 tablespoons arrowroot powder

3 cups lemon goo

Ingredients: Fruit Glaze

1 ½ cups raspberry juice

1 ½ cups raspberry jam

4 tablespoons agar-agar flakes

Fresh pear slices, for garnish

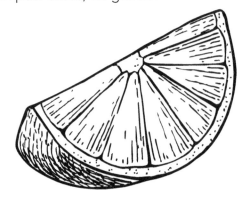

Method: Lemon Goo

1. Add everything, except the rice milk, into a blender and blend well.
2. Add rice milk and blend again.

Method: Tart Crust

1. Grind nuts until fine.
2. Combine oil, rolled oats and maple syrup.
   Add just enough of this mixture to the nuts to moisten.
3. Press into the bottom of a removable-bottom 10-inch tart pan
   and bake at 350°F for 10 minutes.

Method: Tart

1 Dissolve arrowroot powder in water.
2. Heat goo until simmering and cook until agar-agar has dissolved,
   then add the dissolved arrowroot powder.
2 Whisk continuously while bringing back to a boil.
4. Remove from heat and fill the baked tart crust.
5. Let cool and glaze.

Method: Fruit Glaze

1. Simmer all ingredients in a saucepan until agar-agar is
   dissolved, then pour over tart. Let set.
2. Chill in refrigerator for 2 hours.

Garnish with fresh pear slices.

Lemon Lavender Cheesecake

*G-ZEN FAVORITE
(RAW AND GLUTEN-FREE)

Ingredients: Crust

2 cups cashews, raw and unsalted

¾ teaspoon salt

3 tablespoons maple syrup

½ teaspoon vanilla extract

Ingredients: Filling

3 cups cashews, raw and unsalted
   (soaked for 2 hours)

¾ cup almond milk

½ cup lemon juice

1 cup maple syrup

1 ½ tablespoons vanilla extract

⅓ teaspoon sea salt

2 teaspoons dried lavender

¼ teaspoon turmeric, optional for coloring

1 cup coconut oil, melted

Method: Crust

1. In a food processor, add cashews and salt and grind into a fine meal.
2. Add the maple syrup and vanilla and process until combined.
3. Press into a 9-inch springform pan.

Method: Filling

1. Blend all ingredients, except coconut oil, until smooth and creamy.
2. Add coconut oil and blend well.
3. Pour filling over crust and place in freezer to set for 2 hours.
4. Remove from freezer and let sit for 20 minutes or as needed before you serve.
5. Cover and store in refrigerator for 7 to 10 days or can be frozen to store.

This is by far our most popular raw cheesecake on the menu at G-Zen!

Lemon Tahini Dressing

(RAW, GLUTEN-FREE AND NUT-FREE)

Ingredients:

1 cup raw sesame tahini

1 - 2 garlic cloves

2 tablespoons wheat-free tamari or
   coconut aminos

1 - 2 lemons, juiced

½ teaspoon Himalayan sea salt

1 tablespoon coconut nectar, maple syrup or sweetener of choice
   ¼ cup water

Method:

1. In a high-speed blender, mix all ingredients until creamy.

2. Store in airtight container for 5 to 7 days.

This is a great staple dressing. Enjoy on any salad or wrap.

Mango Lime Parfait

(RAW AND GLUTEN-FREE)

Ingredients:

1 - 2 cups raw almonds

3 - 4 teaspoons maple syrup

5 ripe mangos, coarsely chopped

1 cup lemon or lime juice

1 teaspoon lemon or lime zest

4 - 8 dates, pitted

Method: Crust

1. Chop the almonds finely in a food processor or grinder so the consistency is close to almond meal.
2. Gradually add the maple syrup, using just enough for the almond meal to hold together.

Method: Filling

1. Place the mango pieces in a blender and blend until smooth.
2. Add the juice, zest and dates.
3. Keep blending until you achieve a smooth pudding-like consistency.

Assembly:

1. Set out 4 parfait glasses.
2. Put some crust mixture at the bottom of each glass.
3. Add a layer of mango filling.
4. Layer with more crust and continue repeating the layers, ending with crust on the top.
5. Chill if desired.

Top with **Vanilla Cashew Crème** (recipe can be found in this book) and fresh mint.

A PEACEFUL HEART IS A POWERFUL HEART.

Maple-Glazed Coconut Bacon

(GLUTEN-FREE AND NUT-FREE)

Ingredients:

2 tablespoons liquid smoke

2 tablespoons wheat-free tamari,
    or coconut aminos (for a soy-free option)

1 tablespoon coconut oil, melted

2 tablespoons pure maple syrup

1 tablespoon water

3 ½ cups dried coconut flakes

2 teaspoons smoked paprika

½ teaspoon garlic powder

2 teaspoons mesquite powder

1 dash sea salt, to taste, optional

¼ teaspoon black pepper

> Coconut bacon can be stored in a sealed bag or container for up to three weeks in the refrigerator.

Method: Crust

1. Preheat oven to 325°F.
2. Combine liquid smoke, tamari (or coconut aminos), coconut oil, maple syrup and water in a large mixing bowl and whisk together.
3. Pour in coconut flakes and use a wooden spoon to gently toss the coconut oil and liquid mixture with the coconut flakes.
4. Add smoked paprika, garlic powder, mesquite powder, salt and pepper and toss coconut flakes to coat evenly.
5. Once the coconut is evenly coated, pour it onto an oiled baking sheet and place in the oven.
6. Bake for 20 to 25 minutes, using a spatula to flip the 'bacon' about every 5 minutes so it cooks evenly. The coconut bacon will burn, so please check and flip regularly.
7. After baking for 25 minutes at 325°F, you can turn the oven down to 200°F and let the coconut bacon crisp up.
8. Remove from oven when they are brown and crispy.

Let cool and enjoy.

Maple-Glazed Coconut Bacon

Need we say more? A maple-glazed coconut bacon that can be added to everything and anything under the sun. This nut-free, gluten-free, cruelty-free bacon will make your taste buds tingle.

Salads, soups, baked potatoes or virtually anything you can think of, will taste better with this bacon on top of it. Please feel free to add an extra kick to the recipe by adding cayenne powder, more tamari or more liquid smoke. If you choose to make this recipe soy-free and use coconut aminos instead of tamari, we suggest using a bit more liquid smoke than called for in the recipe.

Remember, you are a rock star in the kitchen and you can create any recipe with your signature touches and make it your own.

Marinated Grilled Tofu Steaks

(GLUTEN-FREE AND NUT-FREE)

Ingredients:

1 pound firm tofu, cut into 6 slices lengthwise (non-GMO, locally made is best, we prefer The Bridge Tofu made in CT)

4 tablespoons tamari or nama shoyu, divided

4 tablespoons extra-virgin olive oil

½ tablespoon garlic, chopped

2 tablespoons onion, chopped

2 tablespoons basil, chopped

1 teaspoon tarragon

6 tablespoons apple cider vinegar

6 tablespoons water

Method:

1. Pre-heat the oven to 350°F.
2. Cover the tofu with a mixture of 2 tablespoons tamari, olive oil, onions and garlic and bake on a small sheet pan until browned on all sides.
3. Add the other 2 tablespoons of tamari, basil, tarragon vinegar, and water together to make a marinade.
4. Transfer tofu to a smaller pan and pour marinade over tofu.
5. Refrigerate for at least 12 hours.

Now you can grill, broil or pan-sear your tofu steaks. Whatever method you choose, cook for approximately 10 minutes or until steaks are cooked through and browned.

Serve and enjoy!

Mega-Protein Donut Holes

(GLUTEN-FREE)

Ingredients:

1 ½ cups raw almonds

½ cup rolled oats (gluten-free)

2 teaspoons cinnamon

1 dash sea salt

¼ cup almond butter or peanut butter

2 tablespoons raw sesame tahini

1 - 2 teaspoons hemp protein, optional

3 Tablespoons coconut oil (heated to liquefy)

2 Tablespoons maple syrup or coconut nectar, or to taste

1 teaspoon vanilla extract

Cacao nibs or shredded coconut, optional

Method:

1. In a food processor, pulse the almonds and rolled oats until a flour-like consistency is reached. Add cinnamon and salt and set aside in a mixing bowl.
2. In another small bowl, mix together the almond butter or peanut butter, tahini, hemp protein, liquefied coconut oil, sweetener and vanilla extract. Using your hands or a wooden spatula, mix all the ingredients together and pour wet liquid over dry ingredients. If the batter is too dry, add a small amount of filtered water.
3. Roll the mixture into small donut-sized balls and place onto a plate. As a variation, the donut holes can be rolled in shredded coconut or cacao nibs, before chilling, for extra flavor and a finished look.
4. Place plate in the freezer for a maximum of 10 minutes.
5. Store in an airtight container in the refrigerator.

Mom's Healing Burdock Recipe

by Chef Bun Lai

(GLUTEN-FREE AND NUT-FREE)

Ingredients:

3 burdock roots, peeled and scrubbed

3 large carrots, peeled

2 tablespoons roasted sesame oil

2 teaspoons crushed chili pepper flakes

4 tablespoons maple syrup

3 tablespoons tamari

¾ cup water

Method:

1. Cut burdock root and carrot into 2-inch long matchsticks then soak in cold water.
2. Heat a frying pan with sesame oil and sauté burdock root and carrots for 5 minutes. Add remaining ingredients along with ¾ cup of water.
3. Cover and let simmer over medium heat. When the water has disappeared, the burdock is done.

Kimpira gobo is a traditional Japanese recipe for burdock root. When my brother, Ted, and I were little, we used to forage burdock, and then our mother would prepare it for us using this recipe. European settlers introduced burdock to the Americas and it is eaten worldwide as a vegetable and a detoxifying medicinal herb.

Bun Lai is an internationally recognized food culture innovator known for inventing a plant-based and fully sustainable menu that focuses on using evasive ingredients. His 35-year-old family restaurant, Miya's, in New Haven, Connecticut, was founded by his mother, a nutritionist, and is the first sustainable sushi restaurant in the world.

Not-So-Spanish Gazpacho

by Mimi Kirk

(GLUTEN-FREE AND NUT-FREE)

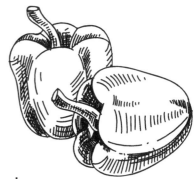

Ingredients:

4 Roma tomatoes, quartered and seeds removed

1 small yellow bell pepper, broken into pieces

1 small sweet red pepper, broken into pieces

1 large English cucumber, cut into chunks

⅛ cup shallots, cut into pieces

2 Fuji apples, cut into chunks and seeds removed

2 tablespoons good-quality extra-virgin olive oil

1 - 2 garlic cloves, crushed or chopped

1 - 2 medjool dates or a small handful raisins

½ bunch mint leaves

½ lime, juiced

Himalayan salt, to taste

Freshly milled black pepper, to taste

Filtered water – start with 1¼ cups and
add more as needed for desired texture

Chopped scallions, thinly sliced radishes,
and avocado for garnish

Method:

1. Place all ingredients, except garnish, into a blender or food processor and mix to desired texture. I like mine just a little chunky, but well incorporated. If you prefer a thinner texture, add a little more water or blend for a longer period of time.
2. Mixture is best if chilled before serving so all ingredients meld well together.

When ready to serve, place in bowls and garnish with toppings.

TIP: Spice it up with chili flakes, jalapeno or chili oil.

Mimi Kirk is an author, raw food chef, international speaker, and health and life coach. She is the author of *Live Raw, Live Raw Around the World,* and *The Ultimate Book of Modern Juicing.*

Perfect Cauliflower Pizza Crust

(GLUTEN-FREE AND NUT-FREE)

Ingredients:

1 medium head cauliflower

½ cup chickpea flour

¼ teaspoon sea salt

1 teaspoon dried basil

1 teaspoon dried oregano

1 teaspoon garlic powder or

1 - 2 teaspoons fresh garlic, minced

1 teaspoon dried rosemary

2 - 3 tablespoons cold-pressed olive oil

Egg replacer or equivalent of 3 eggs

  (**Flax Eggs** can be used; recipe can be found in this book)

NOW THAT'S A PIZZA!

> **Note:**
> You may want to experiment with different types of flours to see which you like best for your crust, or which gives the result you are looking for regarding texture. For a Paleo-friendly option, try almond or coconut flour instead.

For best results, remain open minded that while this is a pizza crust, it is more fragile than regular pizza with a slightly different texture.

Method:

1. Preheat oven to 450°F.
2. Cut stems off the cauliflower and place the florets in a food processor. Pulse cauliflower until it looks like rice. It will take a few batches in the food processor – don't try to fit it all in at once.
3. Put the grated cauliflower into a large saucepan, cover with water and boil until softened and cooked through, approximately 5 minutes.
4. Remove from heat, strain well, place the cauliflower in a dish or pan, and place in the freezer for 5 to 10 minutes to cool.
5. Once it has cooled enough to handle, use a kitchen towel or nut milk bag to squeeze as much water out as possible. Once you think you are done squeezing, squeeze more. *This is the most important step for getting a crispy crust.*
6. Mix the cauliflower in a large bowl with the rest of the ingredients until thoroughly combined.
7. Spread the "dough" onto a greased piece of parchment paper and form 2 smaller crusts, or one larger one. Avoid making the crust too thin as it may crack on the edges.
8. Place the parchment paper on a pizza stone (or baking sheet) and bake for 15 to 20 minutes, or until the edges are brown.
9. Remove from the oven and add pesto, red sauce, vegan cheeze, and any other toppings you choose.
10. Put the pizza under the broiler, on low, for about 3 to 5 minutes, or just until everything is heated through.

Serve with Gratitude and Love.

Cut and serve by the slice. Our favorite way is served deep dish style with a knife and fork.
It is a wonderful substitute when you are hankering for a pizza and since its virtually allergen-free, you can enjoy as often as you like with zero guilt.

Quinoa and Bean Burgers

by Katrina Mayer

(GLUTEN-FREE AND NUT-FREE)

Ingredients:

½ cup shelled raw pumpkin seeds (don't soak)

2 cups cooked quinoa

2 cups cooked beans
 (chick peas and/or cannellini beans)

1 tablespoon tahini

2 tablespoons lemon juice

1 tablespoon Za'atar
 (or any spice blend you like)

2 teaspoons sea salt

Method:

1. Put the raw pumpkin seeds in a food processor and pulse until you have a mixed texture with a few small pieces and lots of powder.

2. Add the rest of the ingredients to the food processor and process until everything is evenly blended. The mixture will be quite doughy and thick.

3. Using a ½ cup measure, scoop out the quinoa and bean mixture. Place scoops of mixture on wax paper and flatten to make burgers. You will get 8 hearty burgers from this recipe.

4. Put some coconut oil in a pan and brown both sides of the burger on medium-high heat. It's about 4 to 5 minutes per side. (Don't undercook them or they won't stay together.)

5. Store any unused quinoa and bean mixture in a covered container in the refrigerator for up to 3 days.

Serve on a bun or on top of a salad. Add a spicy dressing if you like some zing.

Katrina Mayer is an author, blogger and workshop leader. Get more info and additional recipes at **www.KatrinaMayer.com**

Raspberry Apple Crumble

(NUT-FREE)

Ingredients:

3 Granny Smith apples, peeled, seeded and sliced

1 lemon, juiced

2 cups fresh raspberries

1 cup flour

½ cup Florida Crystals® natural sugar

½ cup coconut oil

¼ teaspoon nutmeg

When it's cold outside, there's something therapeutic and invigorating about a fresh fruit crumble. This recipe can be easily made gluten-free by substituting the flour, using gluten-free flour instead.

Method:

1. Preheat oven to 375°F.
2. Peel and core apples and slice each into 8 to 10 pieces.
3. Arrange in baking dish sprayed with vegetable oil and squeeze lemon juice over them.
4. Drain the raspberries and sprinkle them over the apples.
5. Mix flour and sugar in a bowl. Cut in the coconut oil with a knife until the mixture is crumbly. Add nutmeg and cover fruit with this mixture.
6. Bake for about 25 minutes until the top is golden brown.

Serve accompanied with any vanilla non-dairy ice cream.

Recipe donated by Friends of Animals **www.friendsofanimals.org**

Rawesome Falafel

(RAW, GLUTEN-FREE AND NUT-FREE)

Ingredients:

2 cups carrot pulp

1 cup sunflower seeds, soaked for 2 hours and drained

1 cup sesame seeds, ground

2 teaspoons ground flax seed

1 teaspoon sea salt

2 teaspoons lemon juice

3 teaspoons dried oregano

3 teaspoons black pepper

3 teaspoons cumin powder

4 teaspoons olive oil

1 stalk celery, finely chopped

3 tablespoons filtered water, or as needed

Method:

1. Juice enough carrots to make 2 cups of carrot pulp.
2. Process all ingredients together in a food processor fitted with an s-blade until somewhat coarse, but creamy in texture.
3. Portion into falafels of 2 teaspoons each.
4. Dehydrate at 145°F for 2 hours, then lower to 115°F and dehydrate overnight.

Serve falafels on a bed of organic greens with **Garlic Lemon Aioli** (recipe in this book) and a fresh lemon wedge.

1730s Shadle Farm Scene, by Chris Dyer

Photo: Jeff Skeirik aka Rawtographer

About Ami Beach

Ami Beach has been immersed in the world of nutrition and holistic medicine for more than two decades. Ami is an accomplished author, living foods chef, colon hydrotherapist and certified holistic nutritionist. She has been recognized for her work, both nationally and internationally, and continues to inspire people by being a health motivator and sharing her extensive knowledge of natural healing. Featured on NBC, CBS and ABC News, Ami tirelessly advocates for her commitment to nutritionally wholesome food and a sustainable, health-focused lifestyle based on the premise that you are what you eat, drink and breathe. She feels that it is important to take responsibility for one's own health, and her holistic approach includes incorporating the principles of "Food as Medicine," as well as the importance of detoxification of body, mind and spirit.

Ami has continued to deepen her understanding of health and longevity throughout her life and finds great inspiration through her personal mentorship and friendship with *New York Times* best-selling author Anthony William. She considers the "Medical Medium" series to be one the most profound bodies of work available today in the health and wellness arena. Ami credits Anthony for helping inspire her to continue her life's mission and encouraging her to take the plant-based movement to the next level by reaching as many people in the world as possible.

With Chef Mark by her side as her partner and husband, the dynamic duo is ready to conquer the world with their love for one another and passion for spreading awareness about a plant-based and sustainable lifestyle. They split their time between their organic farm in Durham, CT, and a tropical Caribbean oasis in Culebra, Puerto Rico.

Ami is proud to be the head mixologist of custom health elixirs and infused cocktails, as well as the creator of the raw food inspired menu at G-Zen. Ami is also the founder/CEO of Gmonkey mobile, "G-glo Organic Juice Fast" and creator of the "G-glo Total Reboot Program" that has been endorsed by *New York Times* best-selling author Dr. Ann Louise Gittleman, PhD.

Nectar by Ami is her signature botanical perfume line, which she hand-makes and customizes to order.

The complete Nectar product line and the "Total Reboot" 10-day plant-based cleanse are available on line at www.g-glo.com.

If you are in Connecticut, please visit G-Zen's Aroma Bar, which features Ami's top-selling natural fragrances and tonics.

What Does Raw Vegan Food Mean?

A raw vegan diet is made up of fresh, whole, unrefined, living, plant-based foods, including all fruits, vegetables, greens, herbs, nuts and seeds, which are consumed in their natural, unprocessed state.

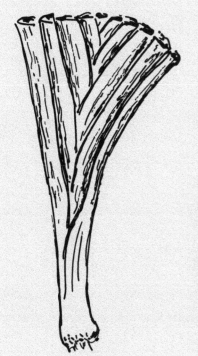

The belief is that cooking foods destroys much of their nutritional value and kills off many of the important enzymes, vitamins and minerals that make our food so healthy for us. Raw foods are often referred to as "living foods" because all of the powerful plant enzymes are kept intact and not destroyed during the cooking process. In a raw foods lifestyle, food is consumed in its natural, raw (living) state and cooking is limited to using a dehydrator or any method that keeps the temperature of the food under 118° Fahrenheit. Keeping foods under 118°F, is believed to retain many of the essential nutrients and enzymes and "vital life force of the food," and this has beneficial effects on the body, organs, metabolism and digestive system.

** Within this book, we use the word "raw" for the purposes of defining the preparation or "un-cooking" of the recipe. We allow for spices, seasonings and other ingredients that may not technically be raw, but for taste purposes and ease of the recipe, we feel it is acceptable since the main components of the dish are in the raw and unprocessed state. Remember, plant-based cooking or "un-cooking" is not about restrictions, but allowing for the magic to unfold.

Salt and Vinegar Chips

(RAW, GLUTEN-FREE AND NUT-FREE)

Ingredients:

2 large zucchini

½ cup apple cider vinegar

½ cup water

1 tablespoon olive oil

1 teaspoon sea salt

Method:

1. Use a mandoline to slice zucchini into thin pieces.

   If you don't have a mandoline, use a knife to slice them thin enough.

2. Add zucchini to a large bowl and cover with apple cider vinegar and water.

   Let them marinate for about 1 to 2 hours. Drain.

3. Massage the olive oil into the veggies and season with salt.

   Place on a dehydrator screen and dehydrate for 4 to 6 hours at 140°F and serve.

Be the Change you want to see in the World.

"Save the Tuna" Salad with Poppy Seed Mayo

(RAW AND GLUTEN-FREE)

Ingredients:

1 cup sunflower seeds, soaked 2 hours and drained

¼ cup of nama shoyu

1 - 2 pinches Celtic sea salt

1 teaspoon cumin powder, or to taste

1 handful fresh cilantro

2 scallions, chopped

2 carrots, peeled

2 celery sticks, chopped

1½ - 2 teaspoons dulse

1½ teaspoons kelp powder

Juice of 1 - 2 lemons

Method:

Place all ingredients into a food processor and pulse for 30 seconds, then scrape down the sides and pulse again. If you need a little water to get the mixture going, add a small amount until it is well mixed, like a traditional tuna salad texture.

Serve on flax crackers, on top of a salad or in a wrap!

This recipe has changed the lives of so many people who crave tuna salad, but want a healthier version that's vegan friendly.

For added amazing flavor and texture, you can use this awesome vegan mayo recipe and add it to the Save the Tuna salad to make it creamier. Or it can simply be used on your salad or wrap on top of the Save the Tuna, just like you would use a traditional mayo.

Poppy Seed Mayo

(RAW AND GLUTEN-FREE)

Ingredients:

1 cup raw cashews, soaked for 2 hours

½ cup water

¼ cup olive oil

3 teaspoons lemon juice

1 teaspoon Dijon mustard

1 teaspoon apple cider vinegar

½ teaspoon sea salt

1 teaspoon poppy seeds

Method:

1. Blend all ingredients, except poppy seeds, together in a food processor.
2. Once a creamy consistency is reached, add poppy seeds.
3. Let firm up in refrigerator and then either mix the mayo with the Save the Tuna salad for extra creaminess, or simply use the mayo as a topping. Either way, it is so delicious and satisfying that this may become a staple dish in your household.
4. Store in an airtight container for 5 to 7 days in refrigerator.

1730s Shadle Farm House, by Chris Dyer

About the historic Shadle Farm
Powered by 100% solar energy

Shadle Farm, originally called the Bates-Newton homestead circa 1730 in historic Durham, CT is a country lovers' rapture, complete with gigantic stone hearths, several barns and stone walls made from reclaimed Newton family barns. A quick stroll to the natural stream at the property's edge reveals a vibrant bed of year-round watercress. An ancient maple flanks the front and flora abounds, with daisies, wildflowers, lily patches, 200-year-old daffodils and endless nasturtium flowers.

This historic 270-year-old farm is the home and sanctuary of Mark Shadle and Ami Beach. The couple has been working hard to restore the property and slowly turn it back into active farmland by planting a wide array of organic fruits, herbs, medicinal plants and vegetables after 30 years of dormancy.

The farm and all of the outbuildings, including a commercial chef's kitchen, are run exclusively on solar energy. The kitchen is the hub of much of the inspiration of the life work that they share.

Many of the organic ingredients for their award-winning G-Zen Gmonkey food truck are grown and harvested at the farm and are incorporated into the seasonally inspired menu. The couple also composts all of the organic waste material from both the restaurant and truck, creating a very nutrient-dense soil for the gardens and growing beds. They are committed to making the restaurant, truck and farm an example of full sustainability and green business practices in every way possible.

Shadle Farm has become a favorite stop for many health and wellness leaders and for anyone interested in seeing first-hand how this couple is living their ultimate dream by sharing their gifts with the world. Mark and Ami hope to be a living example of how creating a life from heart-centered passion and complete dedication to their mission can have a huge impact on the planet and make a difference in the lives of the people they touch along the way.

Shadle Farm Simple Mint Dressing

(RAW, GLUTEN-FREE AND NUT-FREE)

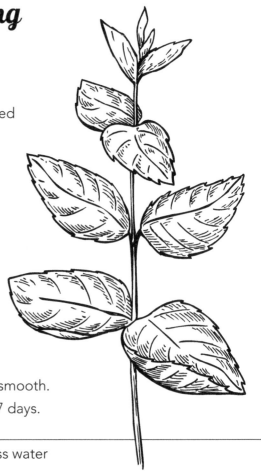

Ingredients:

¼ cup sunflower seeds, best if soaked overnight and drained

½ cup fresh mint

½ white onion or a small bundle of scallions

2 tablespoons raw sesame tahini

2 garlic cloves, minced

1 tablespoon lemon juice

1 tablespoon apple cider vinegar

2 dates, soaked

1 cup water

Sea salt, to taste

Method:

1. In a high-speed blender, mix all of the ingredients until smooth.
2. Store in an airtight container in the refrigerator for 5 to 7 days.

Feel free to adjust the ingredients to taste or add more/less water depending on the desired thickness.

Enjoy this oil-free, low-fat dressing that is a staple of ours at Shadle Farm.

Simple and Quick Hemp Pesto

(RAW, GLUTEN-FREE AND NUT-FREE)

Ingredients:

½ cup organic hempseed

4 - 6 garlic cloves, depending on taste

3 - 5 cups fresh basil

1 teaspoon sea salt

1 teaspoon black pepper, freshly ground

1 cup nutritional yeast

½ cup olive oil

½ cup organic cold-pressed hemp oil

Method:

1. Add all ingredients to a food processor and process until paste forms.
2. Use immediately or pack the pesto into a jar and store in the freezer or refrigerator.

Use on anything like pasta, zucchini noodles, pizza and crackers or as a healthy dip for veggies.

Shadle Farm Wild Dandelion Fritters

(GLUTEN-FREE AND NUT-FREE)

Ingredients:

2 cups unsprayed dandelion flowers, wiped clean

1 ¼ teaspoons sea salt, or to taste

1 tablespoon fresh lemon juice

1 cup gluten-free flour

1 cup fine cornmeal

¼ teaspoon freshly ground pepper

½ teaspoon chili powder

1 tablespoon chopped fresh thyme, or
    1 teaspoon dried

1 ½ teaspoons dried Ener-G® egg replacer
    (found in any health food store,
    follow manufacturer's directions
    for 1 egg)

¼ cup non-dairy milk

2 cups olive oil

Just say "NO" to destroying these beauties and let them flourish in your backyard.

Method:

1. When picking dandelions, pinch blossoms off from top of stems. Fill a medium bowl with 4 cups of cool water. Add 1 teaspoon salt and lemon juice. Place dandelions in the bowl and push them down into the water several times to clean them. Drain dandelions upside down on paper towels.

2. In a medium bowl, sift together flour, cornmeal, remaining ¼ teaspoon salt, pepper and chili powder. Add thyme and mix well.

3. In a small bowl, whisk together egg replacer and non-dairy milk. Pour egg mixture into flour and stir until well combined to form a batter.

4. Pour 1 inch of oil into a 9-inch cast-iron skillet. Heat oil to 375°F. Gently dip each flower into the batter. Carefully place into hot oil; do not crowd. Fry until golden, about 2 minutes, turn, and fry 1 more minute, if necessary. Drain on paper towels. Salt lightly.

Serve hot as hors d'oeuvres or as a side dish with a dipping sauce of your choice like **Garlic Lemon Aioli** (recipe found in this book).

Use this dish as a conversation piece with your friends and family to discuss the importance of dandelions for health and sustainability. Oh, and also how delicious they are.

We are big advocates for raising awareness that dandelions are not just weeds, but are medicinal foods that should never be destroyed by pesticides or cut down because they are perceived as a nuisance. This could not be further from the truth. Dandelions are highly nutritious and have numerous health benefits, including aiding in detoxifying the liver and blood. The plant and its flowers are also one of the first foods that bees are attracted to when they come alive in the springtime looking for nourishment.

Skinny Pancakes

(GLUTEN-FREE AND NUT-FREE)

Ingredients:

1 cup water

1 **Flax Egg** (recipe can be found in this book)
 or equivalent egg replacer

1 ripe banana

1 cup chickpea flour

1 tablespoon baking powder

2 tablespoons arrowroot starch or
 kuzu root starch

1 - 2 teaspoons cinnamon

½ teaspoon nutmeg, optional

½ teaspoon cardamom, optional

1 - 2 teaspoons coconut oil, for cooking

Sliced bananas, for garnish

Method:

1. Place all ingredients into a high-speed blender, Vitamix® or food processor and mix until smooth.

2. Liquefy 1 to 2 teaspoons coconut oil in a heated skillet and pour batter into skillet, forming 4-inch pancakes.

3. Cook pancakes until you see bubbles in the batter. Flip and cook for another few minutes. Allow the pancakes to cook until golden.

Serve with sliced bananas on top and whatever toppings you choose.

If you are looking for a totally guilt-free, allergen-free, gluten-free and nut-free pancake, look no further!

You could literally eat pancakes for breakfast, lunch and dinner and you would stay fit and fabulous.

Slimming Hibiscus Leaf and Goji Berry Sun Tea

(GLUTEN-FREE AND NUT-FREE)

Ingredients:

2 quarts (8 cups) water

¼ cup dried goji berries

½ cup hibiscus flowers

3 tablespoons coconut nectar,
   Grade B maple syrup or stevia leaf, or to taste

2 cinnamon sticks

2 - 4 drops citrus essential oils like lemon,
   lime, blood orange or white grapefruit

1 orange, cut into 8 wedges

1 lemon, cut into 8 wedges

1 handful fresh mint

Method:

1. In a large saucepan, bring the water to a boil; remove from heat.
   Add goji berries, hibiscus flowers, sweetener and cinnamon sticks.
2. Let steep for 25 minutes and cool.
3. Pour in a glass pitcher and add the essential oils. If possible, place
   outside in direct sunlight to soak up the energy from the sun.
4. Whisk for 30 seconds; strain into ice-filled glasses.
5. Add an orange wedge, a lemon wedge and fresh mint to
   each glass; squeeze juice from wedges into strained mixture.
6. Store leftovers in the refrigerator for several days

Hibiscus leaves are famous in the Caribbean for their natural diuretic effects, slimming properties and for cleansing the lymphatic system. Goji berries are known around the world as one of the most potent longevity superfoods. This tea can be enjoyed year round and has miraculous results when consumed daily. It is caffeine-free and not only tastes delicious, but also helps you lose weight.

Smoked Ketchup

(RAW, GLUTEN-FREE AND NUT-FREE)

Ingredients:

½ cup sundried tomatoes, soaked 1 - 2 hours

1 medium Roma (Italian) tomato

4 medium medjool dates or ¼ cup coconut nectar

1½ teaspoons raw apple cider vinegar

2 teaspoons water (from soaking sundried tomatoes)

½ teaspoon sea salt

⅛ teaspoon onion powder

¼ teaspoon garlic powder

¼ teaspoon guar gum, optional

½ teaspoon mesquite powder

Method:

1. Cover sundried tomatoes with water and soak for 1 to 2 hours.
2. Drain sundried tomatoes, reserving 2 teaspoons of the water.
3. Blend the sundried tomatoes, reserved water and all remaining ingredients in a food processor until smooth.

Enjoy as a dipping sauce for our **Crispy Onion Rings** or **Epic Sunshine Seed Burger** (recipes can be found in this book)!

Spicy Flaxseed Crackers

(RAW, GLUTEN-FREE AND NUT-FREE)

> Serve with a fresh guacamole, live hummus or any of our nut cheezes and enjoy!

Ingredients:

2 cups whole flax seeds
   (soaked in water for 30 minutes)

½ cup flax meal

½ cup pumpkin seeds (soaked overnight and drained)

1 cup water (or more depending on consistency)

¼ cup Bragg® Liquid Aminos

4 tablespoons fresh lime juice

1 teaspoon crushed red pepper

1 teaspoon onion powder

⅛ teaspoon cayenne pepper

1 tablespoon garlic powder

1 tablespoon coriander powder

1 tablespoon cumin powder

1 teaspoon chili powder

1 cup fresh cilantro

1 cup fresh tomato, diced

1 cup sundried tomatoes
   (soaked for 1 hour)

Method:

1. Soak the flax seeds in 2 cups of water in a medium bowl for about 30 minutes.

2. Drain the flax seeds using a fine-mesh strainer and place the gelled seeds back in the bowl.

3. In a food processor, mix all the ingredients except for flax seeds and flax meal and mix well.

4. In a large bowl, add the soaked flax seeds to the mixture and slowly add flax meal, while stirring, until dough starts to form. If more water is needed to get the dough spreadable, slowly add more water. If dough it too watery, add more flax meal. Once you get the right consistency, let dough sit covered for 10 minutes.

5. Spread the mixture evenly to the edges and across 2 non-stick dehydrator sheets. Then, score into individual crackers.

6. Dehydrate at 105°F for 10 hours and then peel off the non-stick sheet.

7. Continue to dehydrate on the mesh tray until crackers are completely dry and crispy.

Spicy Tomato Bisque

*G-ZEN FAVORITE
(GLUTEN-FREE)

Ingredients:

2 tablespoons olive oil

1 cup carrots, diced

2 cups celery, diced

½ cup scallions, chopped

2 tablespoons garlic, chopped

1 tablespoon dried basil

4 cups whole tomatoes, washes and diced

2 cups vegetable stock

2 cups almond milk

½ cup tomato paste

2 teaspoons dried red pepper flakes

Salt and pepper, to taste

Method:

1. Heat oil and sauté carrots, celery, scallions, garlic, basil, salt and pepper.

2. Add tomatoes, stock, almond milk, tomato paste and pepper flakes and cook for 20 minutes.

3. Hand blend to make smooth and creamy.

Squash Almond Bisque

*G-ZEN FAVORITE
(GLUTEN-FREE)

Ingredients:

2 tablespoons olive oil

1 cup carrots, diced

1 cup celery, diced

1 cup onion, diced

4 cups butternut squash, diced

1 tablespoon garlic, minced

1 tablespoon ginger, minced

1 tablespoon dried basil

1 teaspoon sea salt

8 cups vegetable stock

2 teaspoons cinnamon

1 cup almond butter

Method:

1. Heat oil and sauté next 8 ingredients for 5 minutes, or until color develops.
2. Add stock and cinnamon and bring to a boil.
3. Reduce heat and simmer for 20 minutes, add almond butter.
4. Remove from heat.
5. Pureé with a hand blender and serve.

This has been a Chef Mark Shadle favorite recipe for more than 20 years and it's a cult classic at this point! It's so nourishing and healthy and is a year-round favorite at home and at G-Zen.

Strawberry Chia Fruit Leather

(RAW, GLUTEN-FREE AND NUT-FREE)

Ingredients:

5 cups strawberries, hulled
1 tablespoon lemon juice
2 tablespoons chia seeds
Stevia, for additional sweetness

Method:

1. Blend the strawberries in a blender with the lemon juice,
   chia seeds and a few drops of liquid stevia.
2. Pour onto a dehydrator sheet lined with parchment paper, place in dehydrator
   and set the temperature to 155°F. Make sure the fruit spread is not too thin or it will
   become crispy and not pliable like fruit leather.
3. Let dehydrate for 6 to 8 hours, or until no longer gooey.

The fruit leather will be done when it is is slightly sticky and flexible.
Another option is to allow the leather to dry longer until it becomes a crisp strawberry
chia cracker that kids will love with almond butter on top.

Kids absolutely love making and eating these rolls-ups. The best part is that moms and dads can
feel good about letting their kids eat as much as they want, so it's a win-win for the whole family.

Stuffed Sunflower Curried Collard Wraps

by Rachel Feldman

(RAW, GLUTEN-FREE AND NUT-FREE)

Ingredients:

2 cups raw sunflower seeds,
soaked overnight and drained

2 teaspoons curry powder

1 garlic clove

½-inch piece of ginger

⅔ cup of water

1 lemon, juiced

1 teaspoon sea salt

1 teaspoon pepper

½ cup shredded carrots

1 large celery rib, minced

¼ cup raisins

Collard green leaves

Method:

1. Add sunflower seeds, curry powder, garlic, ginger, water, lemon juice, sea salt and pepper to a high-speed blender.

2. Blend until smooth. Remove from the blender and add to a mixing bowl. Add shredded carrots, chopped celery and raisins. Mix well and let it set in the refrigerator for at least 30 minutes before serving.

Wash and dry one large collard green leaf. Take a knife and slice the middle vein so the leaf can be easily rolled up. Add a few tablespoons of pâté to the leaf. Top with sprouts, avocado, and cucumber slices if desired. Roll into a wrap and enjoy.

Rachel Feldman is a wellness momma, health coach, and business niche coach. Today, Rachel teaches the same system she used to build her successful health coaching practice to other health and wellness professionals. She's helped more than 8,000 health coaches rock their biz to the next level making the money they deserve.

Rachel Feldman, Owner of **rachelfeldman.com**, health coach and business coach, contributor at *Forbes*, *Huffington Post* and *Thrive Journal*.

Sunflower Seed and Herb Spread

(RAW, GLUTEN-FREE AND NUT-FREE)

Ingredients:

2 cups organic, hulled sunflower seeds,
   soaked 6 - 8 hours

2 garlic cloves

2 teaspoons raw apple cider vinegar

½ lemon, juiced

1 tablespoon fresh parsley, chopped

1 tablespoon fresh dill, chopped

½ cup water

Sea salt and black pepper, to taste

Method:

1. In a food processor fitted with an s-blade,
   mix all ingredients until a nice,
   creamy spread is formed.

2. Store in an airtight container for 5 days.

Enjoy on veggies, wraps or sandwiches as a great alternative to cashew-based cheezes.

Super Seed Parmesan Cheeze

(RAW, GLUTEN-FREE AND NUT-FREE)

Ingredients:

1 cup hemp seeds

½ cup sesame seeds

¼ cup nutritional yeast

1 teaspoon sea salt

½ teaspoon garlic powder

Method:

1. Add all ingredients to a food processor or blender and pulse a couple times until everything is combined.
2. Place mixture in a sealed container and store in the refrigerator for up to 3 weeks.

Sprinkle this mixture on just about everything and anything when you are craving a cheesy flavor. Top off pasta, spaghetti squash, steamed veggies, salads, popcorn, baked potatoes and more.

Each tablespoon adds 6 grams of protein and it's completely nut-free for those who have nut sensitivities.

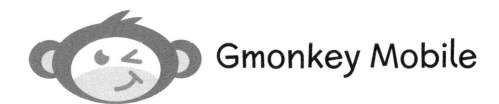

Gmonkey Mobile

Gmonkey was named the "Nation's First Fully Vegan and Sustainable" food truck at its launch in 2011. The eco-truck founded by G-Zen owners Chef Mark Shadle and Chef Ami Beach was catapulted into stardom with its devoted fans since it first hit the streets. We serve "Farm to Street"™ vegan and organic food to the masses at farmers' markets in the Greater Hartford and New Haven, CT, areas and everywhere in between. The multi-award-winning truck has been featured on both the local news and nationally on NBC, CBS, FOX and CNN. It has quickly become a favorite to many thousands of devoted G-monks (fans of Gmonkey) who eagerly wait to hear where their beloved vegan truck will be popping up next.

"The ingredients that go into our dishes are of the same top-notch quality and freshness as the ingredients at fine restaurants, but they are even better because we source 100% organic and local ingredients only for the truck," explains Chef Mark, who has more than two decades of gourmet vegan restaurant experience.

"Our goal is to break any stereotypes of typical street foods and redefine them in a totally green, provocative and innovative way," says Chef Mark.

"We are passionate about delivering fresh, eco-street food that is pure and delicious, and we'll never skimp on the integrity of ingredients or the taste," he says. "We handcraft our food daily from scratch. Our mantra is to serve delicious, healthy and eclectic food that honors the environment and harms not a single animal in the making. Our goal is to make food you love and food that makes you feel good. It's that simple."

The truck runs exclusively on biodiesel fuel that is made from converting organic vegetable oil into a clean energy source. In support of our green initiative, Gmonkey only uses biodegradable, vegetable-based plates, napkins, utensils, etc. They also recycle and/or compost all kitchen food scraps, which are brought back to Shadle Farm, the solar-powered farm in Durham, CT, known as Gmonkey Headquarters.

Gmonkey is available seasonally for catering, weddings, corporate events and fundraisers in the Connecticut area. Our mission is to help spread awareness about the power of plant-based nutrition in any way possible.

We aim to shatter any concepts of typical 'Street Food' and blow people's minds with how plant-based food is actually better tasting than regular street food. The best part is it's 100 times healthier, too.

Voted among the **"Top 5 Vegan Food Trucks in the USA"** by P.E.T.A and featured in VegNews.

Huffington Post named Gmonkey one of the **"Nation's Top Ten Healthiest Food Trucks in America."**

Gmonkey Truck, by Chris Dyer

Sweet Potato Bliss

by Rachel Feldman

(RAW, GLUTEN-FREE AND NUT-FREE)

Ingredients:

2 cups water

2 small sweet potatoes, peeled and cubed

1 yellow pepper

2 stalks celery

¼ small onion

6 fresh basil leaves

½ cup tahini

½ tablespoon garam masala

1 garlic clove

1 avocado

Fresh parsley, minced

Method:

Blend the water and sweet potatoes for 1 minute until smooth.

Add other ingredients and blend. Top with fresh parsley.

Rachel Feldman is a wellness momma, health coach, and business niche coach. Today, Rachel teaches the same system she used to build her successful health coaching practice to other health and wellness professionals. She's helped more than 8,000 health coaches rock their biz to the next level making the money they deserve.

Rachel Feldman, Owner of **rachelfeldman.com**, health coach and business coach, contributor at *Forbes*, *Huffington Post* and *Thrive Journal*.

Sweet Potato Pad Thai

(RAW AND GLUTEN-FREE)

Ingredients:

3 tablespoons almond butter

2 tablespoons tahini

1 tablespoon tamari (gluten-free)

1 tablespoon agave or maple syrup

½ teaspoon chili flakes

1 pinch cayenne pepper

1 teaspoon brown rice vinegar

1 teaspoon sea salt, or to taste

1 teaspoon plum vinegar

½ cup of water

1 large sweet potato, peeled

10 - 12 almonds, chopped into small pieces

Chopped chives or spring onions for garnish

Method:

1. Add all ingredients except almonds into a high-speed blender or food processor. Blend until creamy.
2. Add chopped almonds to add a little crunch to the Pad Thai sauce.
3. Peel the sweet potato and then use a spiral slicer or a vegetable peeler to make long noodles.
4. Add dressing and toss with the sweet potato noodles.

Garnish with chives and mint spring.

Thousand Island Dressing

(RAW AND GLUTEN-FREE)

Ingredients:

½ cup sunflower seeds, soaked 2 - 4 hours and drained

½ cup cashews, soaked 2 - 4 hours and drained

1 red bell pepper

1 - 2 tomatoes

1 cup celery, chopped

¼ cup fresh cilantro

¼ cup fresh parsley

½ - 1 cup filtered water

4 tablespoons lemon juice

2 tablespoons apple cider vinegar

½ cup sundried tomatoes, soaked for one hour and drained

1 pinch cayenne pepper

¼ cup cold-pressed oil olive, optional

Sea salt, to taste

Method:

1. In a high-speed blender, mix all ingredients until smooth.
2. Store in an airtight container in the refrigerator for 5 to 7 days.

Feel free to adjust the ingredients to taste or add more/less water depending on the desired thickness.

Tofu Sour Crème

(GLUTEN-FREE AND NUT-FREE)

Ingredients:

1 - 12-ounce package organic silken tofu

2 tablespoons fresh lemon juice

2 tablespoons umeboshi vinegar

¼ teaspoon sea salt

Method:

1. In a food processor fitted with an s-blade, add all the ingredients and process until smooth.

2. Continue to scrape down sides until ingredients are well mixed and resembles sour cream.

3. Store in airtight container in refrigerator for 5 to 7 days

---

This recipe could easily replace any dairy-based sour cream for a healthier and delicious vegan option.

WE HAVE MORE TO LEARN FROM ANIMALS, THAN ANIMALS LEARN FROM US.

Tomato Sauce

by Katrina Mayer

(RAW, GLUTEN-FREE AND NUT-FREE)

Ingredients:

2 ½ cups organic cherry tomatoes
½ cup sundried tomatoes
1 teaspoon jalapeno pepper, chopped
1 teaspoon ginger, chopped
2 garlic cloves
20 fresh, large, organic basil leaves
1 sweet red pepper, cut into pieces
1 ½ teaspoons sea salt
¾ cup olive oil

Method:

Put all ingredients into a high-speed blender. Just before you're ready to use your sauce, blend for about 1 to 2 minutes. Leave in blender for another 2 to 3 minutes to thicken.

Serve over raw squash or zucchini noodles.

Great on a hot summer day!

Katrina Mayer is an author, blogger and workshop leader.
Get more info and additional recipes at **www.KatrinaMayer.com**

Triple Chocolate Torte

*G-ZEN FAVORITE
(RAW AND GLUTEN-FREE)

Ingredients: Raw Brownie Crust

3 cups walnuts

½ teaspoon sea salt

1 ½ cups raw cacao powder

3 ½ cups pitted dates

1 teaspoon vanilla extract

½ cup maple syrup

Ingredients: Dark Chocolate Layer

3 ripe avocados

2 pinches sea salt

2 tablespoons vanilla extract

¼ teaspoon cinnamon powder

1 ½ cups raw cacao powder

1 cup maple syrup

⅔ cup coconut oil, melted

Ingredients: Milk Chocolate Layer

1 ½ cups cashews, soaked for 1 – 2 hours

2 tablespoons raw cacao powder

1 ½ teaspoons vanilla extract

½ cup raw agave or maple syrup

½ cup filtered water

1 pinch sea salt

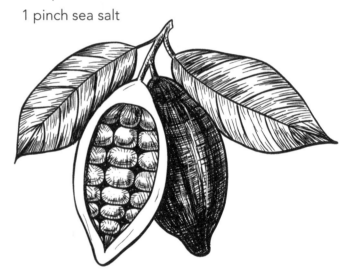

Triple Chocolate Torte Methods

Method: Raw Brownie Crust

1. In a food processor, process walnuts until crumbs form.
2. Add salt and cacao powder and process until just combined.
3. With the processor still on, add dates, one at a time, until they are broken down.
4. Place mixture in a bowl and hand mix in vanilla and maple syrup.
5. Press into the bottom of a springform pan.

Method: Dark Chocolate Layer

1. In a food processor, add all ingredients, except the coconut oil, and process until smooth.
2. Add in coconut oil until well combined. Pour mixture over the raw brownie crust and smooth out evenly. Place in freezer while you finish top layer.

Method: Milk Chocolate Layer

1. In a blender, add all ingredients, except the coconut oil, and blend until smooth.
2. Add in coconut oil and blend until well combined.
3. Pour this mixture on top of the dark chocolate layer.
4. Place in freezer until set, approximately 2 hours.
5. Remove from freezer and let sit for 15 to 20 minutes or as needed before serving.
6. Cover and store in refrigerator for 7 to 10 days or can be frozen.

Tropical Coconut Lime Cheesecake

(RAW AND GLUTEN-FREE)

Ingredients: Crust

1 ½ cups almonds

1 ½ cups coconut flakes

4 ½ tablespoons maple syrup

1 teaspoon vanilla extract

½ teaspoon sea salt

Ingredients: Filling

3 cups cashews, soaked, preferably overnight
   or a minimum of 2 hours

¾ cup lime juice

½ cup coconut milk

1 cup maple syrup

2 tablespoons vanilla extract

⅓ teaspoon sea salt

1 tablespoon coconut oil

¼ cup coconut butter, melted

Method: Crust

1. Process almonds and coconut flakes in
   food processor until broken down.
2. Add in remaining ingredients until
   combined, but do not over mix.
3. Press into bottom of a 9-inch springform pan.

Method: Filling

1. In a blender, blend all ingredients, except
   coconut oil and coconut butter and blend
   until smooth.
2. Add coconut oil and coconut butter and
   blend until well combined.
3. Pour filling over crust and place in freezer
   to set for approximately 2 hours.
4. Remove from freezer and let sit for 15 to 20
   minutes or as needed before serving.
5. Cover and store in refrigerator for 7 to 10
   days or can be frozen.

Turmeric Sunrise

(RAW, GLUTEN-FREE AND NUT-FREE)

Ingredients:

2 large oranges, peeled

1 - 2 tablespoons fresh ginger, chopped

1 - 2 teaspoons turmeric powder
  or fresh turmeric root

1 cup water

1 dash cayenne pepper

Stevia or maple syrup, to taste

Method:

1. In a NutriBullet® or high-speed blender, blend together peeled oranges, ginger, turmeric and water.
2. Add sweetener to taste.

Serve over ice and garnish with an orange slice and dash of turmeric powder on top.

This is a simple yet tasty anti-inflammatory beverage that packs a lot of healing power for both the digestion and the organs. Enjoy a glass of sunshine in the morning and reap the benefits of this nutrient-dense juice.

The Ultimate Un-Chicken Salad with Avocado Mayo

(RAW AND GLUTEN-FREE)

Ingredients:

4 cups raw almonds

5 stalks celery, diced

6 green onions, thinly sliced

2 teaspoons fresh parsley, chopped

5 teaspoons lemon juice

2 dashes cayenne pepper

1 medium garlic clove, crushed

1 ½ teaspoons Celtic sea salt

1 - 2 teaspoons nori dulse flakes, or to taste

Method:

1. Coarsely chop almonds in food processor and set aside.

2. In a medium bowl, combine the rest of the ingredients.

3. To complete, mix in **Avocado Mayo** (see recipe next page) and chopped almonds. Adjust the amount of Avocado Mayo in order to achieve the creamy consistency of "chicken salad" or to desired taste.

Avocado Mayo

Ingredients:

1 cup pine nuts or macadamia nuts, soaked for 1 hour

1 large, ripe avocado

1 teaspoon lemon juice

2 teaspoons apple cider vinegar

1 teaspoon Celtic sea salt

6 medium pitted, dried dates, chopped

½ garlic clove, crushed

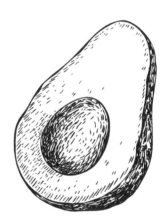

Method:

1. Mix all the ingredients in a food processor until creamy.
2. Add to the Un-Chicken Salad ingredients and serve chilled.
3. Store in an airtight container for 5 to 7 days in refrigerator.

Vanilla Bean and Lacuma Pudding

(RAW AND GLUTEN-FREE)

Ingredients:

1 cup cashews

2 cups water

1 vanilla bean, scraped

2 teaspoons vanilla extract

¼ teaspoon sea salt

¼ teaspoon cinnamon powder

2 tablespoons lacuma powder

½ cup grade B maple syrup

½ cup chia seeds

Method:

1. Blend all ingredients except chia seeds in blender until smooth.
2. Pour in a bowl, add chia seeds and mix well.
3. Place bowl in refrigerator for 1 to 2 hours, stirring every 20 minutes until a pudding-like consistency is reached.

Garnish and serve pudding in approximately 4 glass or parfait dishes. Tastes even more amazing with **Vanilla Cashew Crème** (recipe on the following page) and cinnamon on top.

Lacuma powder comes from a type of fruit native to Peru and South America. Long used as a natural sweetener, it is also used to add a rich caramel flavor to foods, desserts and beverages. However, because it is considered to be a superfood, praised for its adaptogenic qualities and extremely beneficial for health, we use it generously in our recipes both at home and at G-Zen. It is incredibly rich in nutrients including beta-carotene, vitamin B3, iron, zinc, calcium and magnesium.

Vanilla Cashew Crème

(RAW AND GLUTEN-FREE)

Ingredients:

2 cups raw cashews, soaked for 2 hours and drained

½ cup almond milk, hemp milk or water

½ cup maple syrup, or more to taste

1 tablespoon vanilla extract

1 vanilla bean, scraped

2 pinches sea salt

Method:

1. In a high-speed blender or food processor, blend all ingredients until smooth and creamy.
2. Store in an airtight container for up to 10 days in refrigerator.

This recipe can be used in place of whipped cream in any recipe of your choosing.
It is quick and easy and so delicious.

Vanilla Hemp Mesquite Milk

(RAW, GLUTEN-FREE AND NUT-FREE)

Ingredients:

1 cup organic raw hemp seeds

1 tablespoon mesquite powder

1 teaspoon vanilla extract

3 - 4 cups water

Liquid sweetener, to taste

   (stevia, coconut nectar or maple syrup)

Method:

1. Combine raw hemp seeds, mesquite, vanilla and ½ of the water in a high-speed blender. Blend until mixture begins to get creamy and smooth.
2. Slowly add the remaining water and sweetener. Blend for another moment.
3. Chill for 1 hour before serving.
4. Store in an airtight container in the refrigerator for 5 to 7 days.

Mesquite pod powder is a fabulous thickener. It can replace an egg in a recipe for pancakes, waffles or quick bread. It has an amazing unique, sweet flavor! It is considered a superfood from Peru and is a great source of potassium, zinc, sulfur, calcium and magnesium.

Mesquite is excellent over granola and hot or cold cereal and is absolutely delicious and nutritious.

"White Lies, Skinny Pasta"

(GLUTEN-FREE)

Ingredients:

4 medium zucchini, peeled

1 pint cherry tomatoes

1 - 2 tablespoons cold-pressed olive oil or coconut oil

Salt and freshly ground black pepper, to taste

3 tablespoons pesto

2 - 3 garlic cloves, minced

2 tablespoons **Cashew Parmesan Cheeze** (recipe found in this book)

2 - 3 fresh basil leaves

Pine nuts, for topping

Method:

1. Using a spiralizer or a julienne peeler, make long noodle strands with the zucchini, stopping when you reach the seeds. Set aside.
2. Place tomatoes onto a rimmed baking sheet and drizzle with olive oil. Sprinkle with salt and pepper and bake at 400°F for 15 to 20 minutes.
3. Combine the zucchini noodles, a dash of olive oil and pesto, tossing until well coated.
4. Lightly sauté zucchini noodles and garlic in a skillet over medium heat for 4 to 5 minutes.

Top with **Cashew Parmesan Cheeze**, a few chopped tomatoes, fresh basil leaves and pine nuts.

Enjoy "White Lies, Skinny Pasta" with zero guilt and zero grains.

Wild Blueberry and Goji Parfait with Crumble Topping

(RAW AND GLUTEN-FREE)

Ingredients: Parfait

16 ounces frozen wild blueberries

1 ½ cups goji berries

1 tablespoon chia seeds

1 - 2 drops liquid stevia

1 cup raw cashews,
   soaked preferably overnight
   or a minimum of 2 hours

1 tablespoon raw coconut oil

1 lemon, juiced

2 tablespoons maple syrup or
   sweetener of choice

½ teaspoon vanilla bean scraped,
   powder or extract

1 teaspoon maca root powder

2 tablespoons spring water

Ingredients: Crumb topping

½ cup walnuts

¼ cup dates

¼ cup shredded coconut

¼ cup raw oat groats, optional

½ teaspoon vanilla extract

½ teaspoon cinnamon

1 dash of cardamom, optional

1 pinch sea salt

Method: Parfait

1. Mix frozen blueberries and goji berries together.
   Place in refrigerator overnight to allow the blueberries to defrost.
2. Place the mixed berries in a blender with chia seeds and stevia
   and blend into a smooth "blueberry pudding."
3. Process cashews in a food processor until finely chopped.
   Add coconut oil, lemon juice, sweetener, vanilla,
   maca and water. Process until creamy.

Method: Crumb Topping

Pulse the walnuts and dates briefly in a food processor, then add the rest
of the ingredients and pulse lightly to combine into a crumble.

Assembly:

In 3 or 4 glasses, put a dollop of blueberry pudding. Follow with **Vanilla Cashew Crème**
(recipe can be found in this book). Top each layer with crumble. Repeat until all of the pudding,
crème and crumble are finished. Garnish with goji berries. Serve immediately or chill.

Wild Watercress and Daikon Roll with Horseradish Ginger Dressing

(GLUTEN-FREE AND NUT-FREE)

Ingredients:

1 tablespoon fresh garlic, chopped

2 tablespoons sesame oil

4 cups fresh watercress, wild harvested is best

4 large purple cabbage leaves, blanched

1 cup daikon, shredded

½ cup **Wild Horseradish Ginger Dressing**
   (see recipe next page)

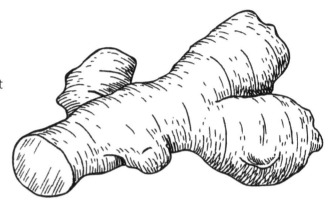

Method:

1. Sauté garlic in oil. Add watercress, stir and wilt down, then cool.

2. Lay cabbage on cutting board and lay watercress and daikon on top.

3. Put 1 to 2 tablespoons of the dressing on top.

4. Roll up tight like a sushi roll and slice into 1-inch sushi-like rolls.

Serve cut side up showing contrast of colors, making a dramatic presentation.

Wild Horseradish Ginger Dressing

Ingredients:

1 garlic clove

1 - 2 teaspoon horseradish, fresh ground

¼ medium onion

1 carrot, peeled and grated

1 ½ tablespoons fresh ginger, peeled and grated

¼ teaspoon powdered mustard

1 teaspoon wheat-free tamari

½ cup sesame oil

½ teaspoon toasted sesame oil

¼ cup brown rice vinegar

1 teaspoon apple cider vinegar

½ cup apple juice

Method:

In a high-speed blender, place all ingredients and blend until smooth.

Horseradish is known in folk medicine as a cure all for many health ailments and is very beneficial for the immune system. Also, it helps remove harmful free radicals from the body and may help protect it from cancers, inflammation and infections. Wild horseradish root and wild watercress are highly nutritious and have many medicinal properties. Any time you can wild harvest or forage for your own wild ingredients, we encourage you to do so. These powerful foods can be sourced in the spring throughout North America.

Eat your medicine and free your soul.

Zen Alive Sour Crème

(RAW AND GLUTEN-FREE)

Ingredients:

1 cup raw cashews or macadamia nuts,
  soaked overnight

¼ cup fresh lemon juice

1 teaspoon raw apple cider vinegar

¼ teaspoon sea salt

2 teaspoons nutritional yeast

1 - 2 capsules of probiotic
  (simply open and empty capsule into recipe mix)

½ cup water or fresh coconut water

4 tablespoons rejuvelac, optional

** Rejuvelac is a non-alcoholic fermented liquid made from sprouted grains. Because it is fermented, rejuvelac contains beneficial bacteria and active enzymes, and thus it is reported to improve digestion of food. There are tons of wonderful rejuvelac recipes online to explore.

Method:

1. Place all ingredients into a high-speed blender.
2. Blend on high for 3 to 4 minutes, scraping down the sides
   as needed, until very smooth and creamy.
3. Put the sour crème into an airtight container.
4. Chill in refrigerator for at least 2 to 3 hours before serving.

It will keep well in the refrigerator for several days.

This is fantastic over raw wraps, as a dip for raw veggies or flax crackers.

GRATITUDE UNLOCKS
THE FULLNESS OF LIFE.

Zen Warrior Immunity Tonic

(GLUTEN-FREE AND NUT-FREE)

Ingredients:

½ cup horseradish, peeled and diced

½ cup garlic, peeled and diced

½ cup onion, peeled and diced

¼ cup ginger, peeled and diced

¼ cup turmeric, peeled and diced

1 habanero chili, split in half

2 oranges, quartered and thinly sliced crosswise

1 lemon, quartered and thinly sliced crosswise

½ cup parsley, chopped

2 tablespoons rosemary, chopped

2 tablespoons thyme, chopped

1 teaspoon black peppercorns

1 teaspoon horseradish

2 to 3 cups raw, unfiltered apple cider vinegar (at least 5% acidity)

¼ cup liquid sweetener, or more

Method:

1. Place all ingredients, except vinegar and sweetener, in a clean 1-quart jar. (We love to use mason jars.)

2. Fill the jar with vinegar, covering all the ingredients and making sure there are no air bubbles.

3. Cap the jar. If using a metal lid, place a piece of parchment or wax paper between the jar and the lid to prevent corrosion from the vinegar.

4. Shake well.

5. Let the jar sit for 3 to 6 weeks, shaking daily.

6. Strain the vinegar into a clean jar.

7. Add sweetener and store in refrigerator for up to a year.

Drink 1 to 2 ounces daily, especially during cold and flu season.

Zucchini Pesto Zoodle Bowl

(RAW AND GLUTEN-FREE)

Ingredients:

1 garlic clove

1 tablespoon pine nuts (or blanched almonds)

1 large handful fresh basil leaves

2 tablespoons lemon juice

2 medium ripe avocados

1 tablespoon olive oil

1 tablespoon water, or more, as needed

¼ teaspoon fine-grain sea salt

Ground black pepper, to taste

6 medium-large zucchini

1 cup cherry tomatoes, halved

Method:

1. In a food processor, combine garlic, pine nuts and basil and pulse to mince.
2. Add lemon juice, avocado, oil and 1 tablespoon of water.
   Process until completely blended and creamy, stopping to scrape down the bowl as needed.
3. If it's too thick, add more water, one tablespoon at a time. Add salt and pepper to taste.
   Always feel free to adjust seasoning based on your taste.
4. Using a spiralizer, create zucchini noodles. If you don't have a spiralizer, use a regular
   vegetable peeler to vertically peel long, thin strips of the zucchini. This will form more of
   a wider "noodle" from the zucchini, like fettuccini.
5. You can lightly sauté the zoodles or choose to leave them raw.
6. Transfer zoodles to a large serving bowl, add pesto and halved cherry tomatoes and mix well.
   Top with **Cashew Parmesan Cheeze** (recipe can be found in this book) for added flavor.

Serve immediately!

YOU WILL NEVER FIND
PEACE OF MIND UNTIL YOU
LISTEN YOUR HEART.

Equipping Your Raw Kitchen

When embarking on a raw journey or simply wanting to incorporate more raw foods into your diet, we all have the same question on our lips: **How can we best equip our kitchen?**

What follows are recommendations based on our personal experiences both at home and at G-Zen. Please bear in mind that each person's needs/ preferences may vary. For instance, we LOVE food prep and concocting gourmet meals, and therefore really appreciate the flexibility that a dehydrator gives for creating different tastes and textures. However, if you're not the culinary type and enjoy very simple and quickly prepared meals, you'll probably find that a good-quality blender, a food processor and perhaps a spiral slicer will be everything you need.

Before we take off on a shopping spree, let's stop for a moment and talk about budget.

Outfitting your kitchen without going broke...
You may or may not have a huge budget to play with, but we suggest that investing in good-quality tools will pay off in the long run. Even if you have to space your purchases out a bit to eventually collect all of the appliances, it's better to wait and get quality items that you will be happy with and love for years to come. Here are a few tricks that have been helpful along the way.

5 tips to save money while equipping your raw kitchen
1. Look for sales and rebate coupons at stores like Bed Bath & Beyond®, etc.
2. Look for refurbished items.
3. Shop on eBay® — a fab place for items new or used.
4. Look at the classified ads in local papers and on Craigslist®.
5. Browse through garage sales and thrift stores. You will be amazed at all the cool stuff to be found!

Raw foodies' best friends

Although you may find most of the tools listed in this book already lying around your kitchen, some will take on a new importance with the raw diet. There are also a few specialty items that will greatly complement your raw culinary adventure.

Blender

We feel that the best place to start is with the single most used appliance in our kitchen: the blender. It runs a minimum of 30 to 40 times a day, sometimes more if we are making sauces, spreads or desserts.

For many years we had a "regular" blender such as a KitchenAid®. While it would puree soft fruits and veggies, it didn't do a fantastic job at it. And with the sort of use a blender gets around here, it generally didn't have a very long lifespan either, and we had to replace it periodically. Finally, it was time to invest in a "real beast"– a high-speed blender. Having had to replace blenders every couple of years at the most, the prospect of spending $300 or $400 on a machine that would last us for many years to come seemed like the way to go. It boiled down to either the Total Blender by Blendtec® or the Vitamix® 5000. Both appliances are very highly rated by the raw food community.

In the end, the 7-year Vitamix® warranty on ALL parts is what sealed the deal versus all the competitors on the market.

And so we went with the Vitamix® 5000 and we have never looked back. The Vitamix® is elegant, easy to use and reliable, and the textures of soups, smoothies, etc. are unreal! There is really no comparison and we couldn't survive without several between home and the restaurant.

It's a wonder how we did without it all these years at home and at G-Zen and we will never go back!

Juicer

There are many different juicers to choose from depending on what you're looking for and what kind of budget you have. For daily juicing, we suggest the Breville® Juice Fountain Elite, a centrifuge system with pulp extraction. It has two different speeds and is super easy to clean up, which is absolutely essential, otherwise you'll find yourself not using it as much as you'd like to because it's just "too much work."

Another great feature of the Juice Fountain Elite is its extra-wide food chute. It can even take in whole apples and lemons! This means you don't have to chop food into smaller pieces, therefore saving a LOT of prep time. We own several juicers either at home or at G-Zen that range in price, from $200 to $2,000, including the Norwalk hydraulic juice press (used exclusively for our fresh-pressed juices and our G-glo juice fasts).

We also love our Champion and Green Star® juicers, especially for juicing dark leafy greens.

However, for the average person, we have found the Breville® Juice Fountain Elite all stainless steel is the most user-friendly and the one we most recommend to clients based on performance and its great value.

As our friend Dave the "Raw Food Trucker" likes to say, "the best juicer is the one you will actually use."

Food processor

Another "must have" in any raw kitchen is a food processor. It is useful for chopping veggies in a snap and making anything from spreads to crackers, nut cheezes, cashew gelato and many of our famous in-house raw cheesecakes at G-Zen. Again, there are tons of models to choose from and varying price tags. The consensus from our culinary team is that the Cuisinart® 14-cup commercial-grade, stainless

steel unit is an outstanding quality, highly reliable machine and is our first choice at G-Zen. On the downside, they can be quite pricey, so it depends on what you're looking for and what kind of money you are willing to spend.

Our recommendation is that this investment in a higher-end Cuisinart® is worth every penny. It will take a beating, keep on going and will pay for itself in the long run.

You might want to consider getting a smaller food processor to start with, or in addition to a full-sized unit, called the "Cuisinart® mini". Not only is it super handy when you don't have a lot of food to process, but it's also more economical. The Cuisinart® mini is something we use at home just about every day and highly recommend it.

Dehydrator

Our top pick is the Excalibur® Dehydrator. It is absolutely the best for the buck. You can find others that are cheaper, but they usually only have heat from the bottom of the unit (which means you need to rotate the food), no fan and no self-timer (dehydration times are much longer with a high risk of fermentation). Excalibur is also available in 5 trays, but in our experience, go with a 9 tray and you will be happier in the end. We also prefer the all stainless steel version, but that is a personal choice.

Spiral slicer

Here's a little gadget that will allow you to make beautiful vegetable pasta in no time at all. Our all-time favorite is the Benriner Cook Helper. It produces perfect "pasta" every single time and gives the flexibility of choosing between three sizes of pasta noodles: angel hair, spaghetti and fettuccine noodles.

Additionally, it allows you to slice vegetables (such as turnips, jicama or beets) very thinly in order to make ravioli wrappers. We use this tool, or one like it, at home and at G-Zen daily to really transform so-so meals into something spectacular.

You can now buy it on Amazon for around $30 to $40. Awesome investment with a great return!

Mandoline or V-slicer

This is an awesome kitchen tool that will help you create uniform veggie slices. It comes in particularly handy for making chips and zucchini noodles for lasagna, or for julienning vegetables for sushi.

One of the main concerns while looking for a mandoline is safety. As you know, these babies tend to be razor sharp, and it wouldn't take much to hurt yourself unless you have a good finger guard. We use a shred-proof cutting glove when we have lots of veggies to slice to avoid any cuts or injury. Mesh gloves are available online or at any retail cooking store.

At-home nut milk maker

This is a kitchen that may not be absolutely necessary, but we have found it to be life-changing in so many ways. Thanks to the recommendation of our raw food rock star friend, Mimi Kirk, we purchased the Soyabella milk maker and we can make gallons of raw, fresh almond, hemp and cashew milk literally in minutes. The cleanup is a snap and it revolutionizes the way you think of nut milk and your average store-bought varieties.

Just try it and you will know what we are talking about. The Soyabella milk maker can also be found online, at Amazon and at other local retailers.

Odds and Ends

As you know, there are all kinds of smaller gadgets and tools that are essential to any kitchen. Indispensable tools include, but are not limited to:

- Knife – a good, sharpened knife is invaluable
- Cutting board
- Measuring cups and spoons
- Grater
- Small citrus squeezer
- Strainers
- Garlic press
- Vegetable peeler
- Various shaped pans – for making lasagna, cobblers, pies, cupcakes, etc.
- Springform pans – for making cakes, raw pies and tarts
- Nut-straining bag
- Glass storage containers
- Kai Boi slicer
- Coconut opener, like Coco Jack for removing the coconut meat easily from fresh Thai coconuts

All of these items and more of our favorite products and recommendations for a vegan lifestyle are available at **http://www.g-glo.com/g-glo-shop/amis-amazon-store/**

About Chris Dyer

Chris Dyer is a Peruvian artist, who lives in Canada and travels the world half of his time. He experiences different cultures and then incorporates them in his own vision of oneness. He serves as a bridge builder among various art movements from skateboard graphics, to visionary paintings, to street art murals and more. He wants to break boundaries and see everything as one optimistic reality. Though his subject matter is as varied as his style, his art is just a reflection of his personal spiritual journey. For more, look out for his coffee table book and his documentary or look him up at www.positivecreations.ca.

While visiting Shadle Farm, Chris Dyer has spent time relaxing and being nourished by the food of G-Zen and Chefs Mark Shadle and Ami Beach. He was very excited to offer original sketches that were inspired by the incredible nature and green mission of G-Zen. And he is thrilled to have his work included in this very special recipe book that is a collaboration of L.O.V.E in its purest form.

About Vasilisa Romanenko

Vasilisa Romanenko is an illustrator, painter and designer. Inspired by nature, fashion, folk art and children's books, she brings her visions to life with paintings of trees, animals and beautiful women. Vasilisa earned her Bachelors of Fine Arts in Illustration at the Fashion Institute of Technology in New York City. Together with her mother, she owns and operates Palette Art Studio in Woodbridge, CT, where she teaches painting and drawing to students of all ages.

She is thrilled to be working with Ami and Mark on capturing the essence of their sustainable mission at G-Zen and Shadle Farm. Her artwork depicts the beauty of Shadle Farm and its plant-based mission on the inside cover of "*Peace Begins on Your Plate.*"

G-Zen has been recognized by a wide range of organizations and publications

Travel + Leisure magazine: "Top Ten Upscale Vegan Restaurants in America"

Nature Conservancy: "Green Plate Award" for CT's Most Sustainable Restaurant

Happy Cow: "World's Top Vegan Restaurants"
(G-Zen is featured in their cookbook, which is available for purchase at the restaurant)

Huffington Post: "Top 10 Vegan Restaurants in America"

Shape magazine: "Top Ten Vegan Restaurants in America"

Yankee magazine: "Top Vegetarian Restaurant in CT & Best Vegan Brunch in CT"

P.E.T.A & VegNews: "Top 5 Vegan Food Trucks in America"

Friends of Animals: "Top 8 Vegan Restaurants in America"

CTNOW New Haven: "Best Vegan/Vegetarian in CT"

Connecticut Magazine: "Best Vegan/Vegetarian Restaurant in CT"

Links and staying in touch

To find out more about our online plant-based detox programs or to sign up for our **FREE** vegan recipes and lifestyle tips, visit **www.g-glo.com** and sign up for our free "Inner glo" membership.

To learn more about our award-winning vegan food truck, visit **www.gmonkeymobile.com**.

To read more about G-Zen and our green mission, visit **www.g-zen.com**.

For information about one-on-one health coaching, vegan lifestyle sessions or group classes, visit **www.amibeach.com**.

To learn more about plant-based cooking demos and events at Shadle Farm visit **www.shadlefarm.com.**

f Facebook: @shadlefarm

◎ Instagram: Ami Beach (amibeach_lifestyle) and Chefmarkshadle

Also stay connected on:

f Facebook: @g-zenrestaurant

◎ Instagram: Gzenrestaurant

🐦 Twitter: gzenrestaurant

Media/Press contact:
email: Shadlefarm@gmail.com

Go vegan

"Peace, Love and Vegan"

A portion of the proceeds from the sale of this book will be donated to various animal welfares organizations, animal rescues and animal charities in both Connecticut and in Puerto Rico.
Thank you for helping us support our vision by purchasing this special book.
Together we can make a difference!

Recipe Notes >

Recipe Notes

CPSIA information can be obtained
at www.ICGtesting.com
Printed in the USA
JSHW020435021020
8440JS00001B/12